THE SMITHS

LAWRENCE WATSON

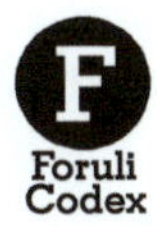

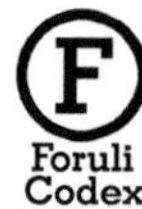

Published by Foruli Codex

FIRST EDITION

ISBN 978-1-905792-45-0

Edited by Karl French

A CIP catalogue record for this book is available from the British Library

Design by Andy Vella, www.velladesign.com

Typeset in Futura

Printed by Lightning Source

Foruli Codex is an imprint of Foruli Ltd, London

www.forulicodex.com

THANKS to my my beautiful family and friends who helped along the way, the Smiths for letting me take the pictures and making such great and lasting music, and Matt, Andy and Karl at Foruli for making me dig those negs out of their dusty boxes.

love and peace

Lawrence

x

SHOOTING THE SMITHS

I think my brother had written the first live review of The Smiths, and I saw them but I didn't take pictures. The first commission was the cover shot for *City Limits* magazine at Morrissey's flat in Kensington. I did a few *NME* covers and when he went solo I did some work for EMI, the "Interesting Drug" cover and other things. I did have an affinity for them. It was simple really because I loved their music – they were one of the great bands of that period, and I appreciated Morrissey's song-writing, his lyricism and his wit right from the start. He gets accused, then and still now, of being depressing and maudlin but you listen to the lyrics and there's a wit there, a sense of humour that maybe goes over a lot of people's heads around the world. Because it's very English and British, with a bit of a Noel Coward and Oscar Wilde tone and also that very Northern thing that maybe doesn't get picked up in some places. I thought that was great and the Northern aspect was very important because when I was starting out as a photographer a lot of good, interesting music was coming from the North: Manchester, Liverpool, and even Barnsley and Bradford with Danse Society and Southern Death Cult and all those indie bands. There were a few things going on in London but it was really happening up there, so we were drawn there.

In my early days I was quite shy and I'd maybe used the camera as a way of becoming invisible, which isn't a bad thing for a photographer of course. By the time I worked with The Smiths I'd become more confident. But even then, when I'd learned my craft, it was important to remain anonymous. I was always conscious of not disturbing the scene and being a big egotistical photographer who comes in with all their baggage and changes the whole feel of a session. It was always more softly, softly with me and making people comfortable and normally that way you get them at ease and get the natural pictures. Of course there was always a lot of thought that went into the process, into the lighting and composition, learning to fill the frame and that was how it always was with The Smiths. They were easy to work with and with them, as with every subject, it's about thought but also looking for and being ready for that lucky moment, that one shot from a roll of film when the light does fall just right. It's about learning to react to that moment, that 1/250 of a second that you're capturing. Morrissey understood that and I got on well with him. He had strong ideas, but that was part of the strength of The Smiths. He saw the whole image and he always saw the importance of photography as reflected in all their sleeve art. He put a lot of thought into the people who'd appear on those. He'd always think of locations when we went up to Manchester, in fact the shop that we used for the last *NME* cover, the Albert Finney shop on the Oldham Road, he'd seen that and saw it fitted with the band. That was one of my favourite sessions with them. I also loved the one with the gravestone and the banjolele. He was one of the subjects that are good for photographers because he'd always put real thought and creativity into the whole process. I still enjoy hearing them – their music stands the test of time, as all great song-writing does. They evoke a period but they last beyond that period. But looking back at them I'm just still really pleased that I got to document that band at that time.

LAWRENCE WATSON

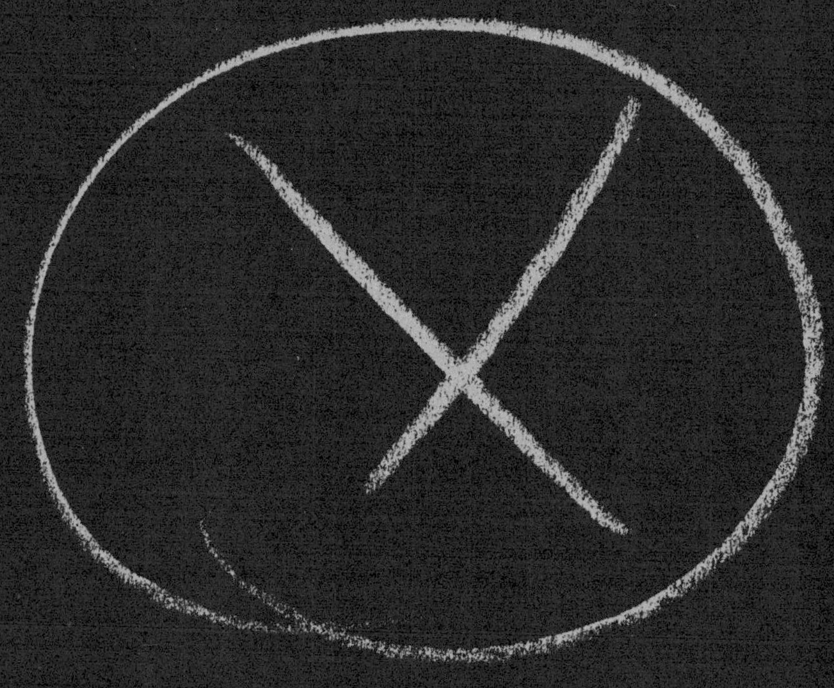

The Smiths and me on the Oldham Road for an *NME* cover session.

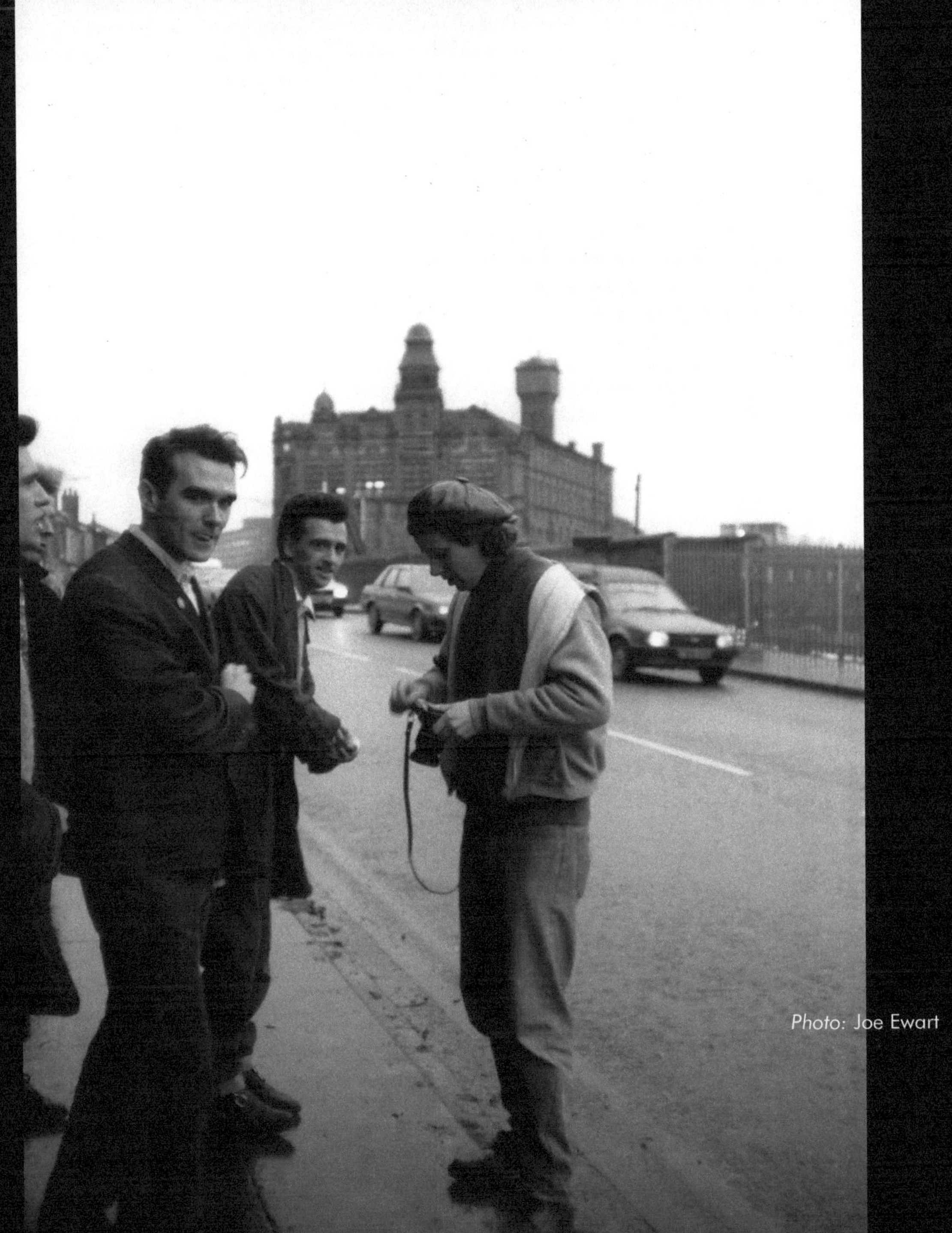

Photo: Joe Ewart

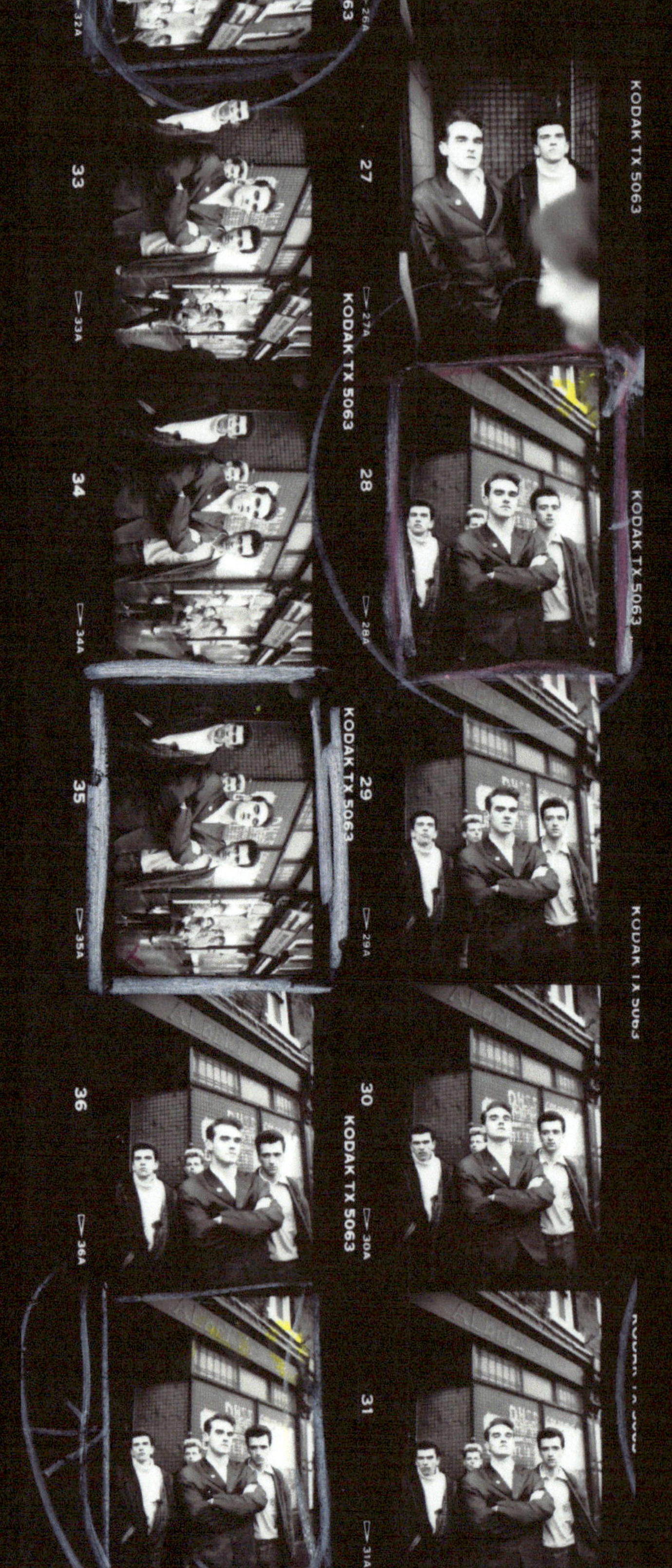
KODAK TX 5063
27
28
29
30
31
33
34
35
36

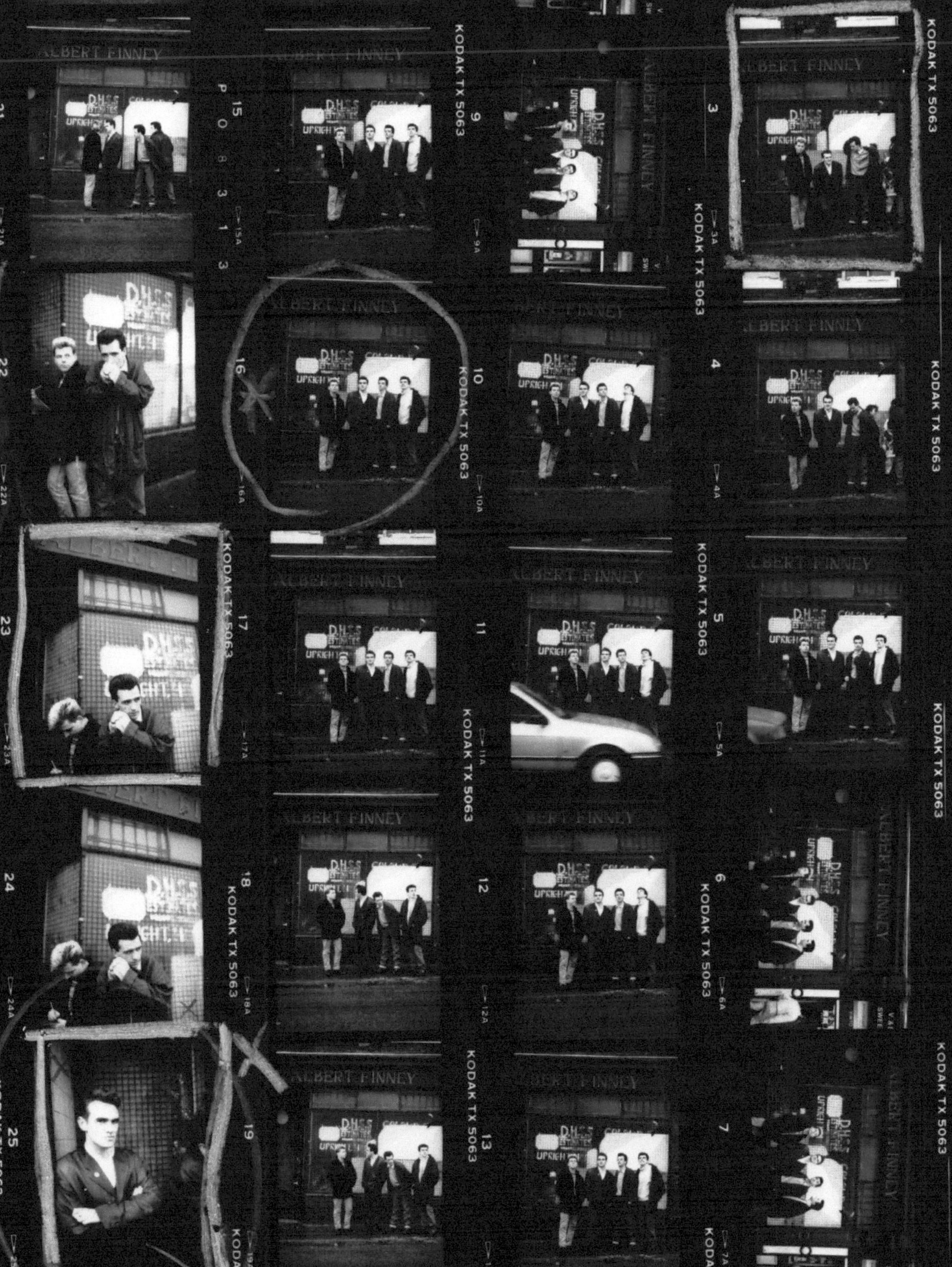
ALBERT FINNEY
D.H.S.S
KODAK TX 5063

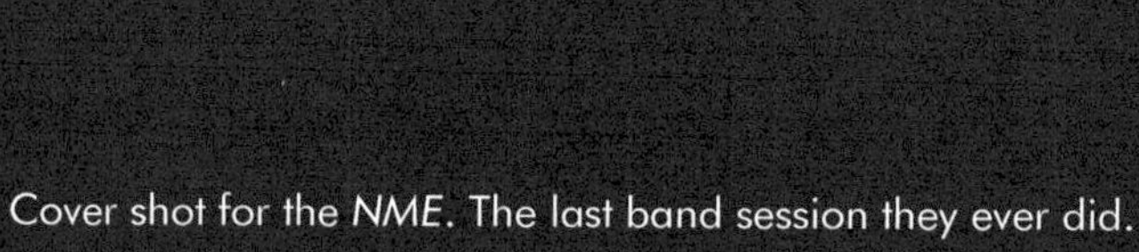

Cover shot for the *NME*. The last band session they ever did.

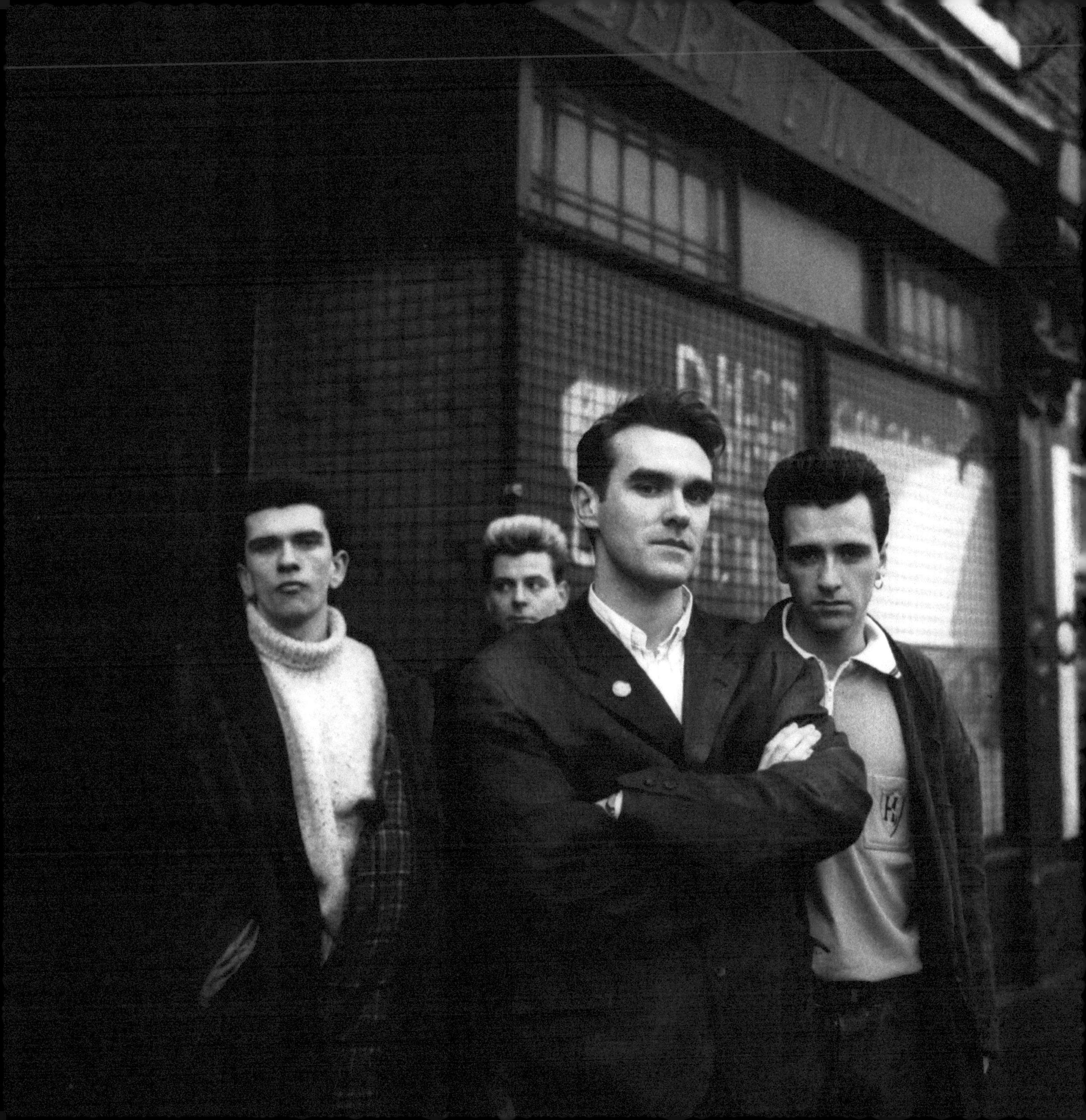

Outside the Albert Finney store - another strong location from Mr Morrissey.

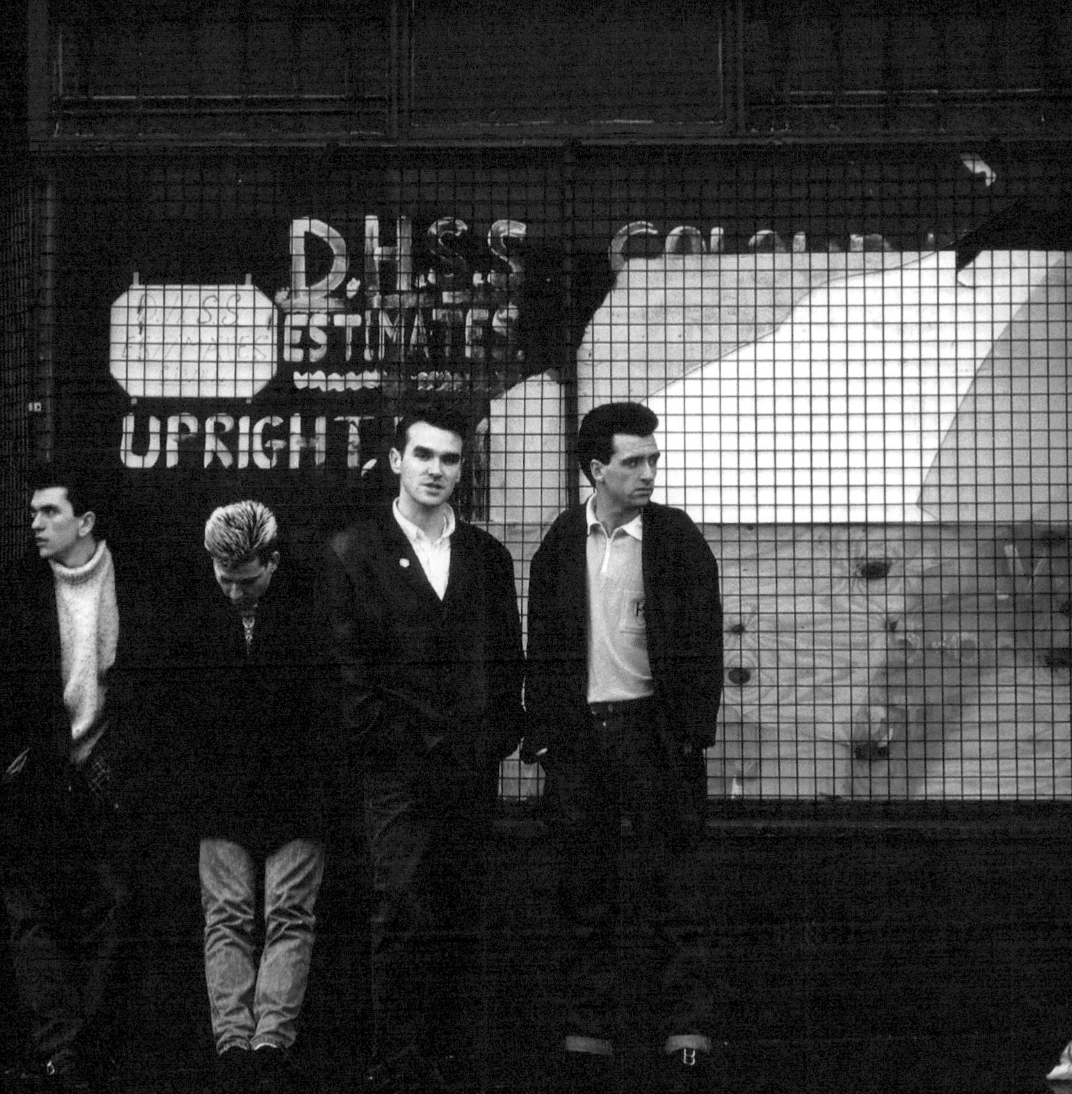
ALBERT FINNEY
D.H.S.S.
ESTIMATES
UPRIGHT

Handsome devil.

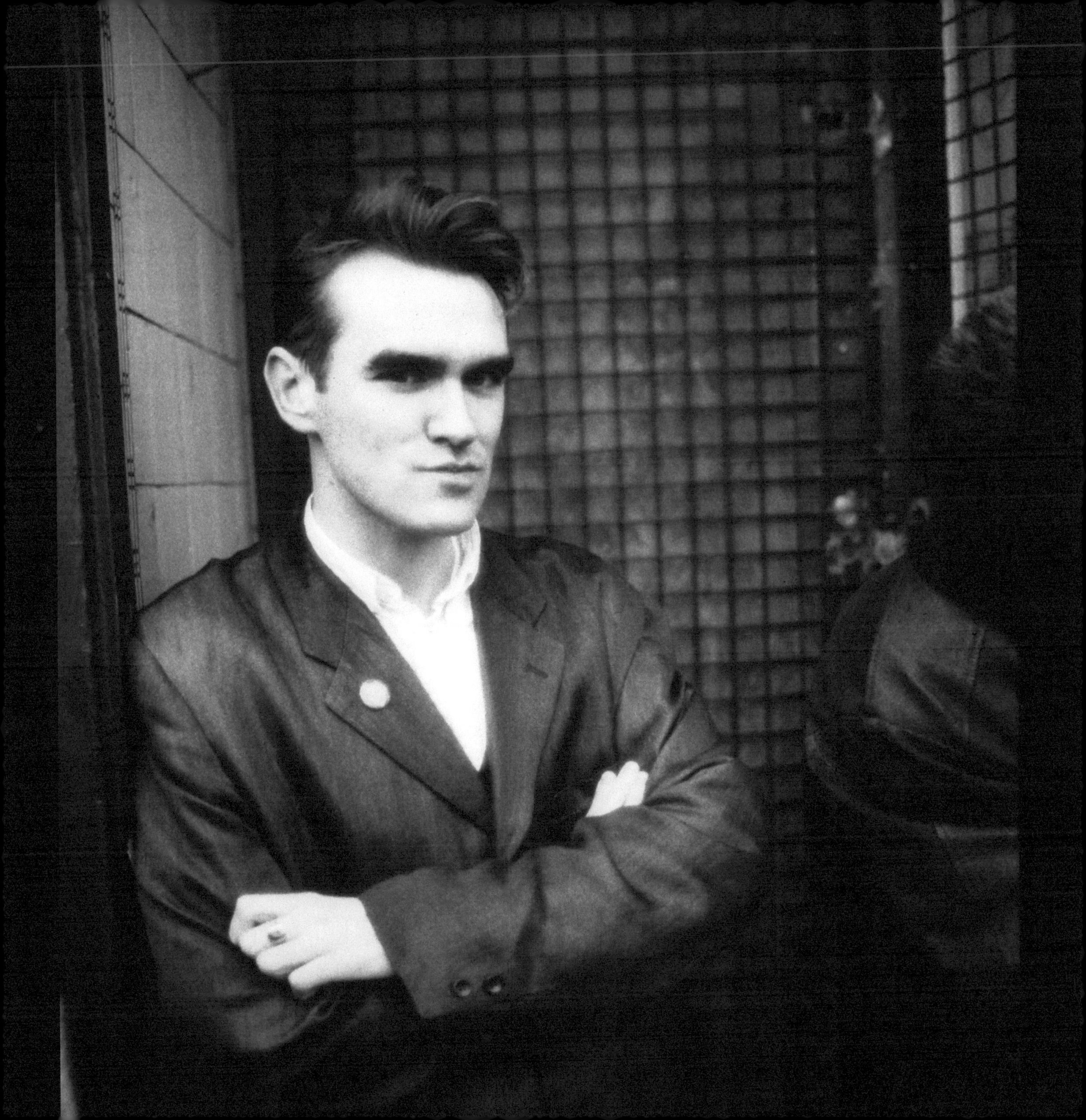

Morrissey and Viv Nicholson of *Spend, Spend, Spend* fame and the cover star of "Heaven Knows I'm Miserable Now".

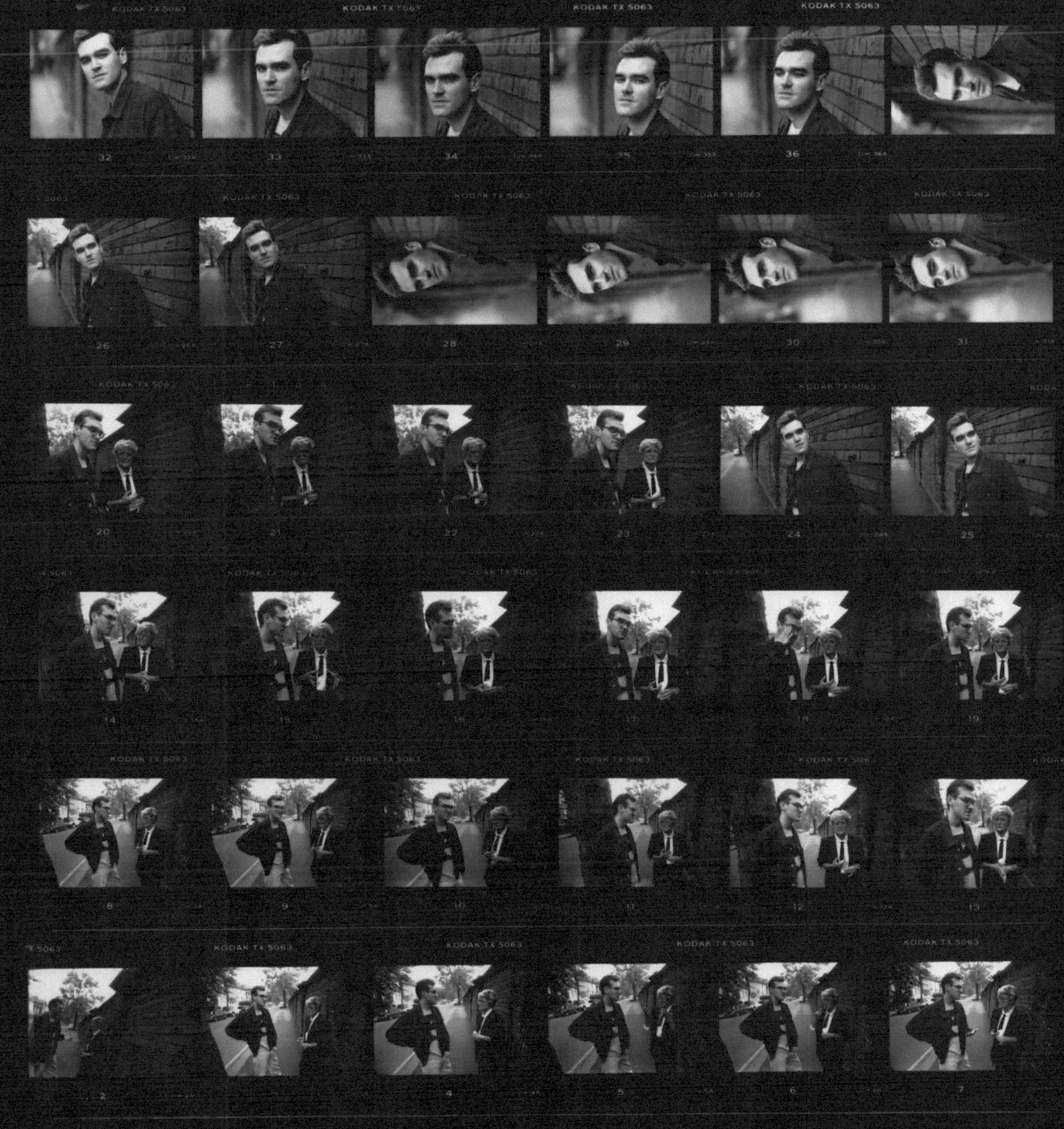

Morrissey and Viv Nicholson in Westbourne Grove, London.

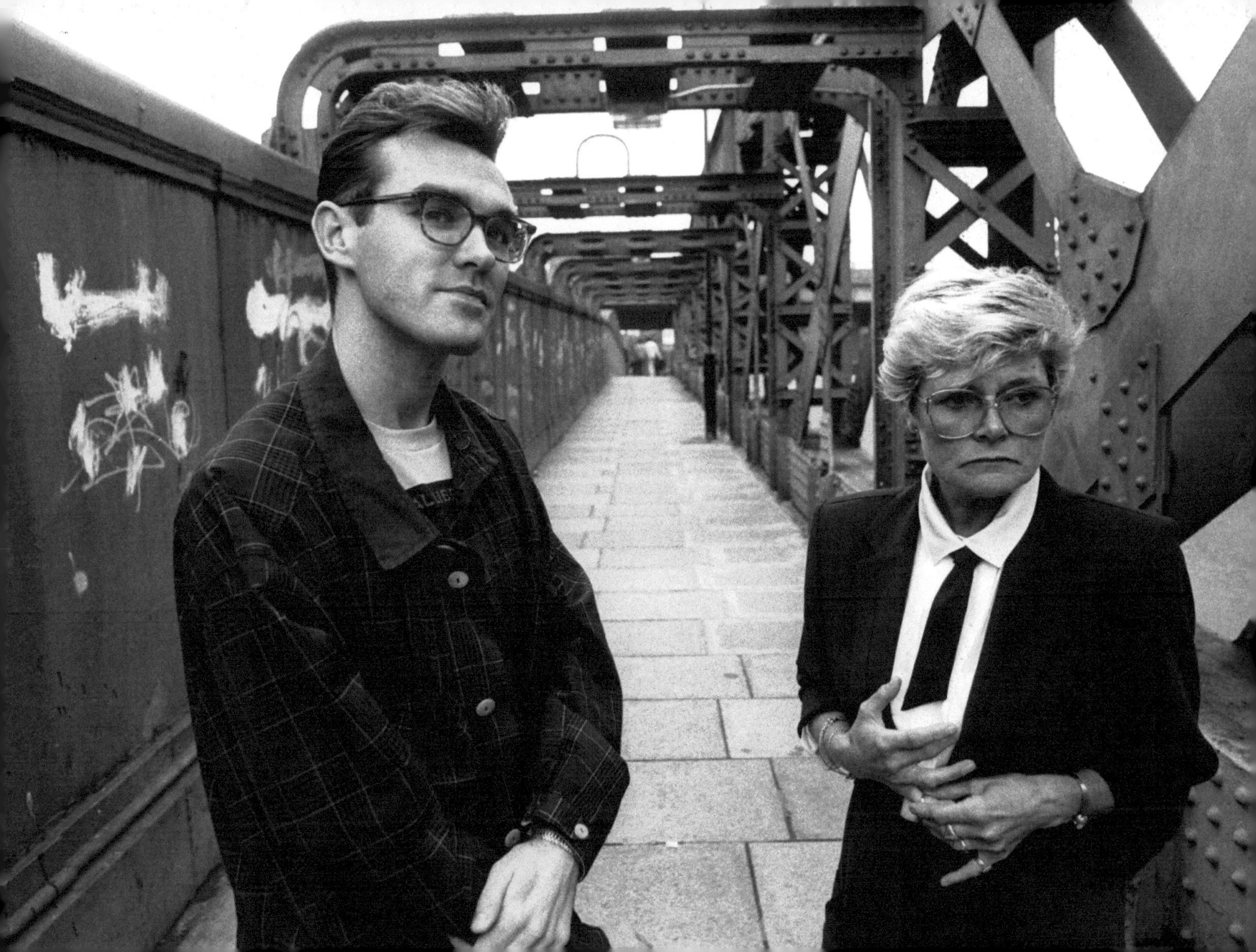

Morrissey in London.

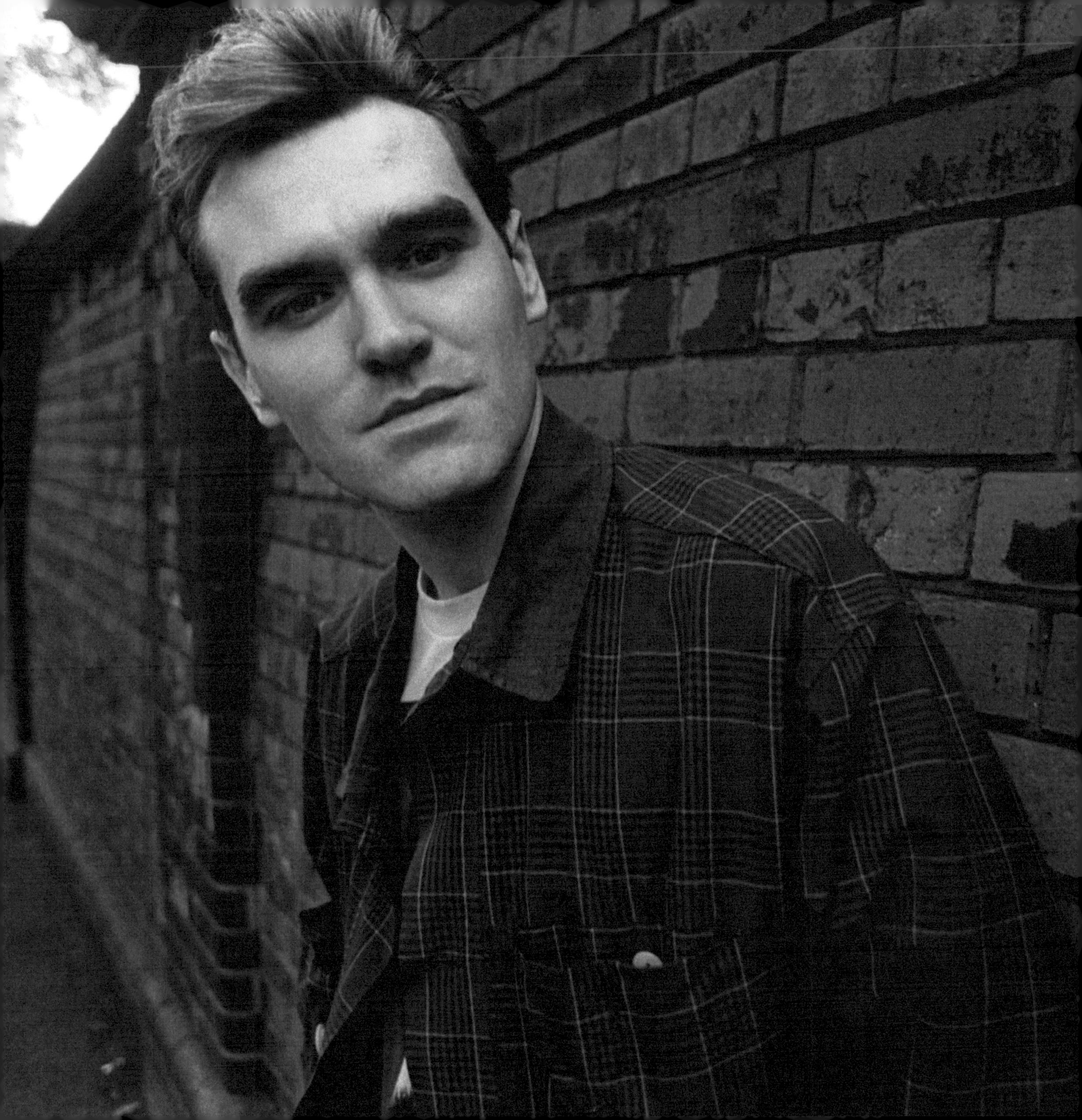

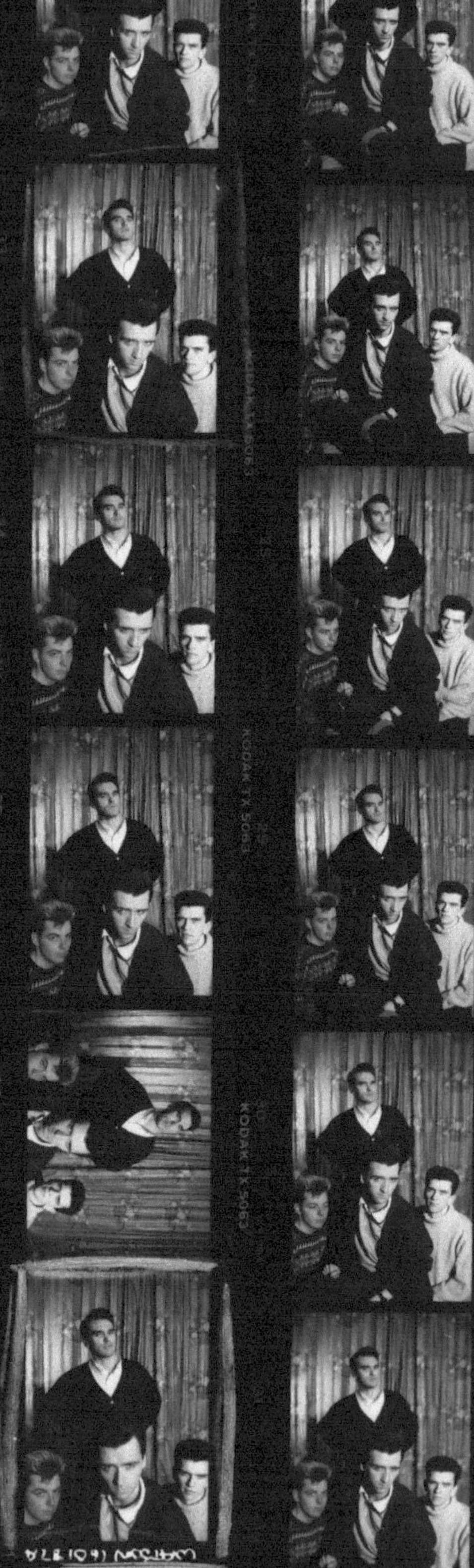

NME cover shoot in the Piccadilly Hotel, Manchester.

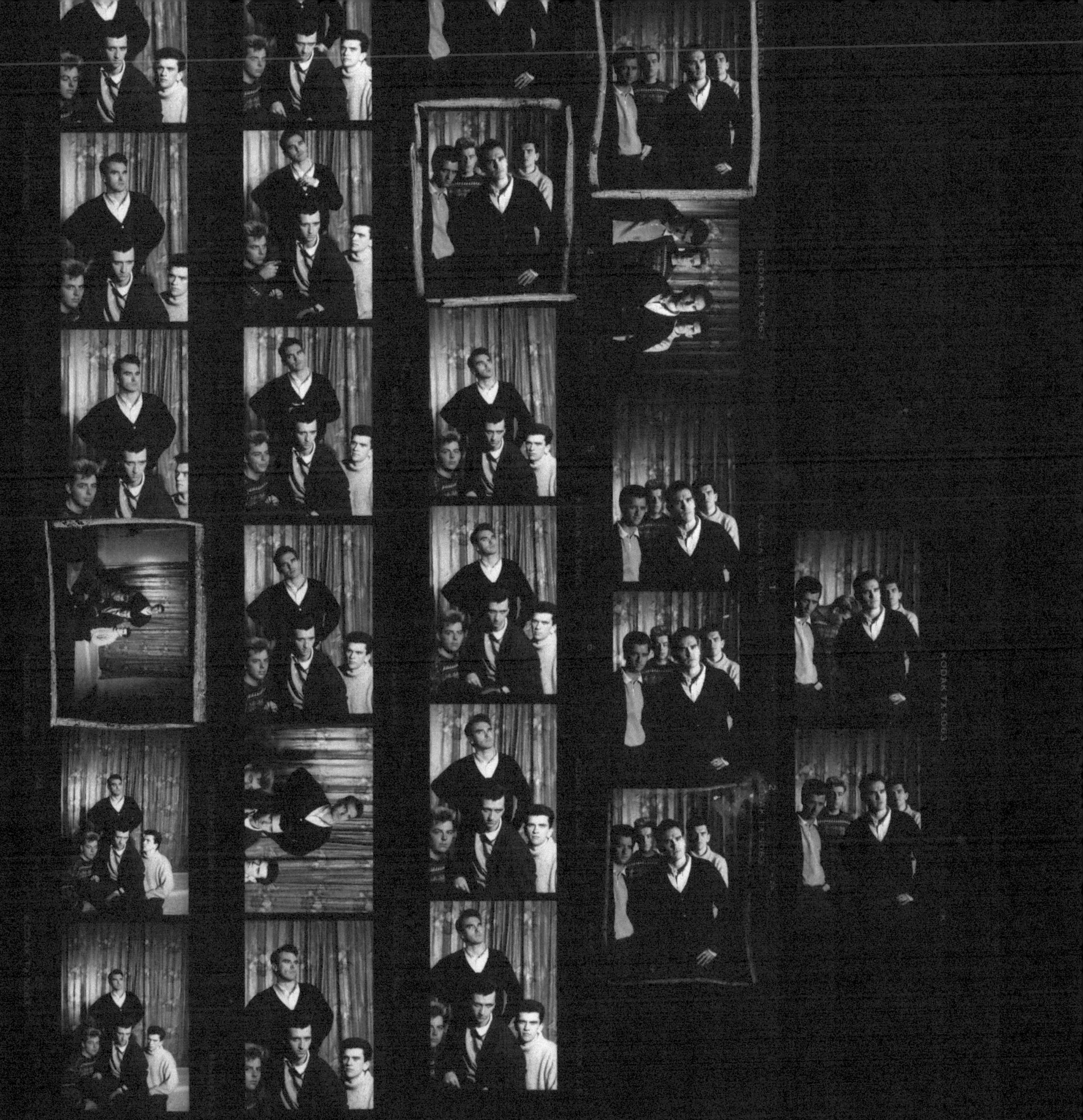

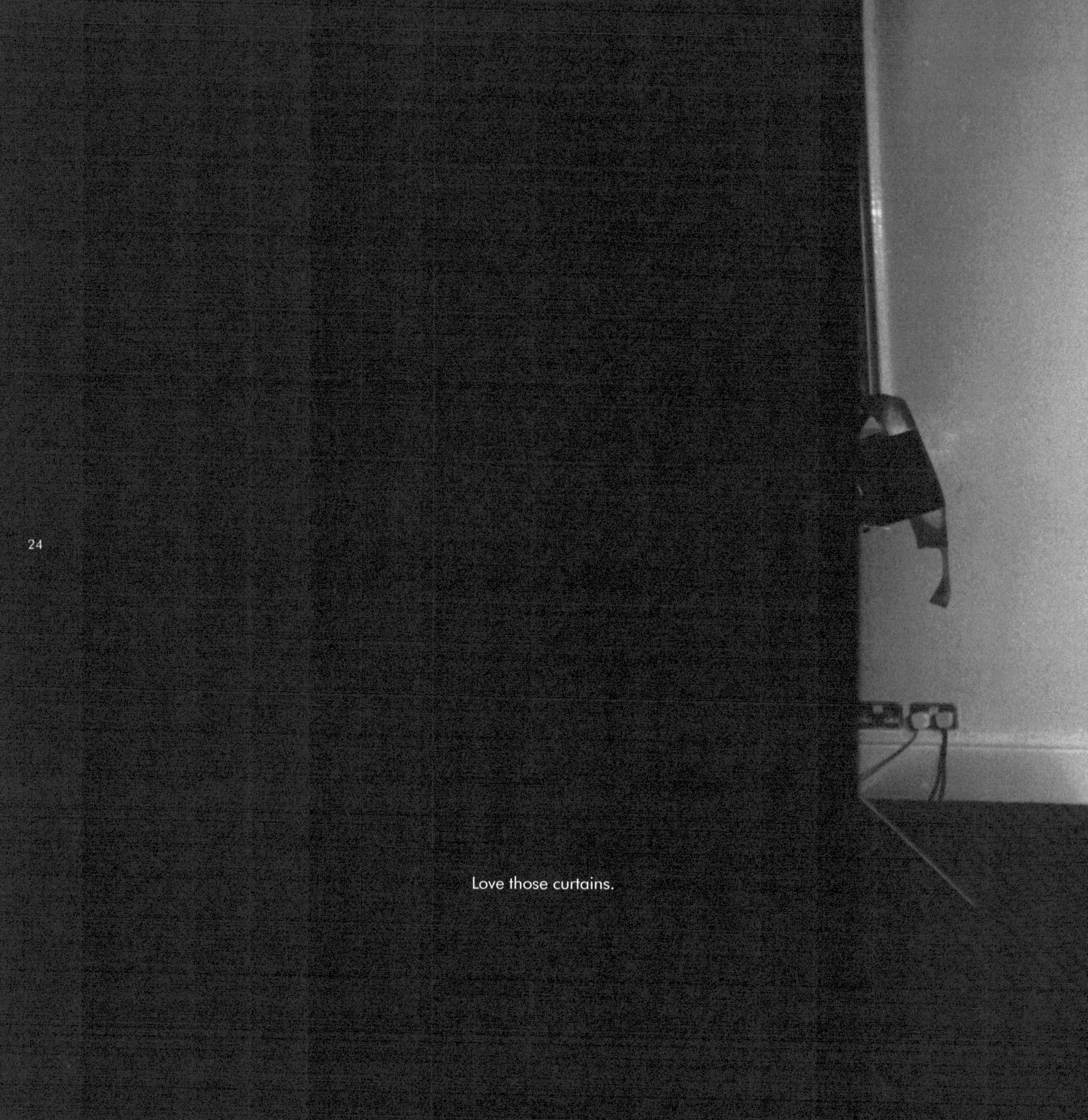

24

Love those curtains.

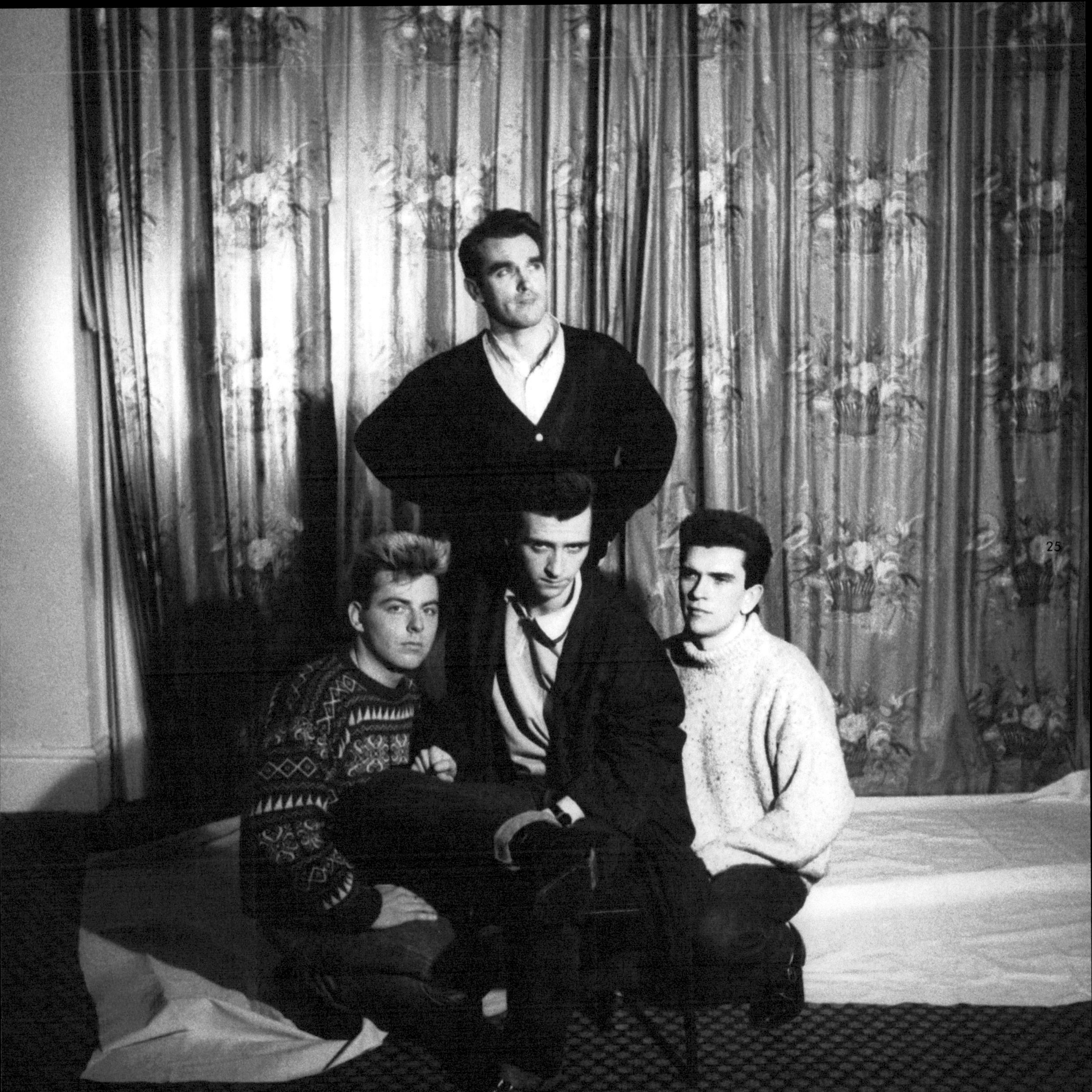

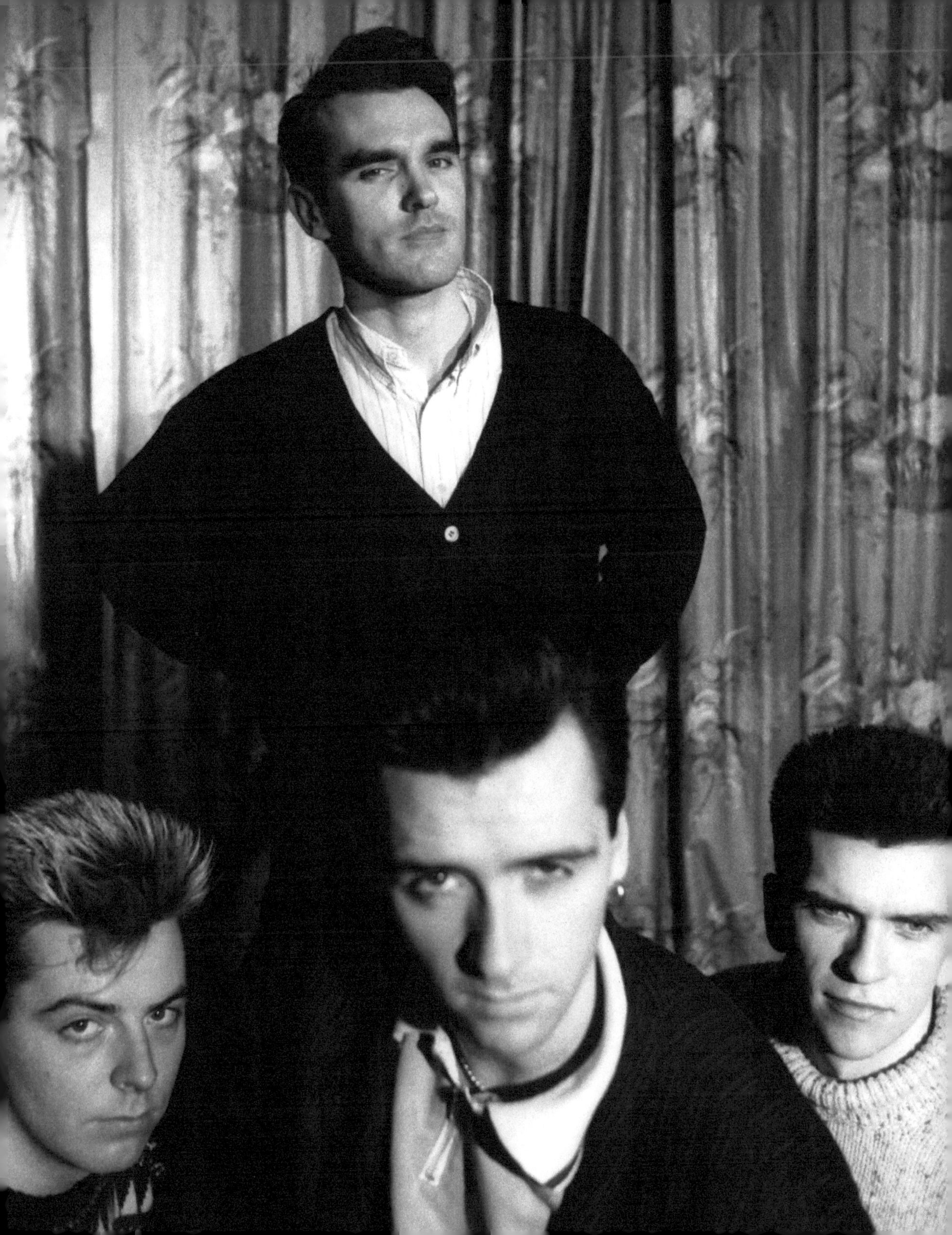

28

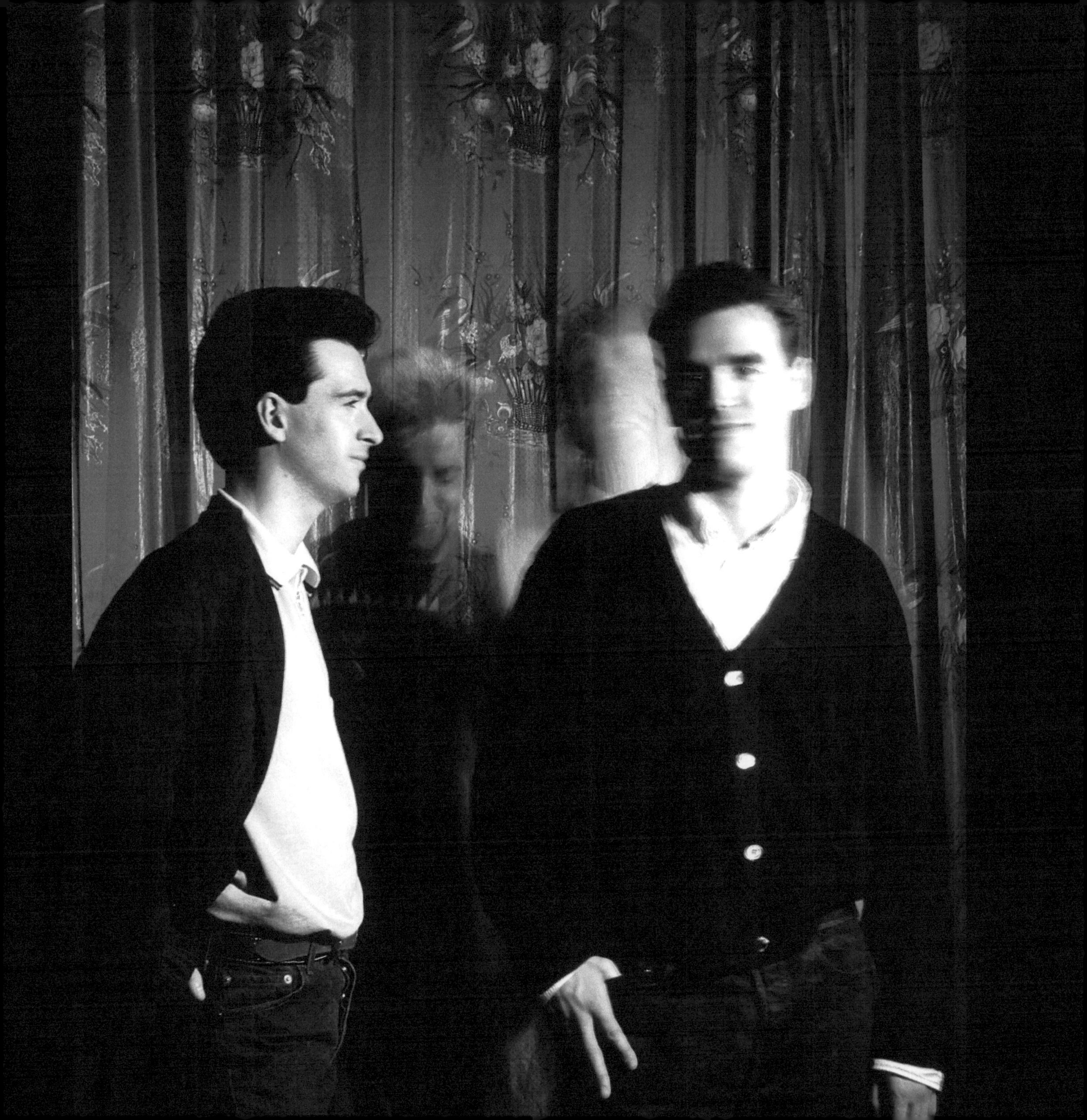

More shots in the Piccadilly.

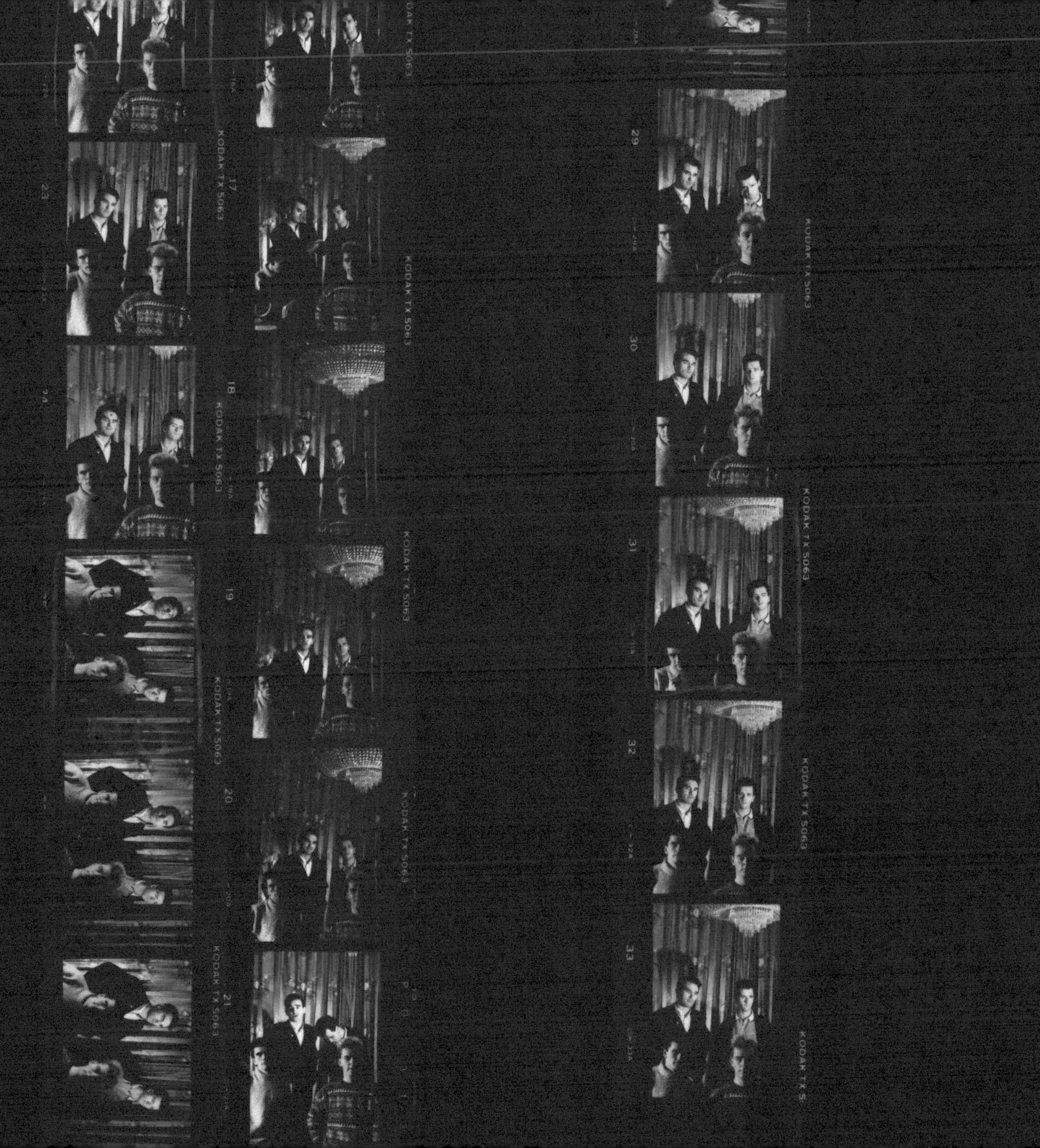

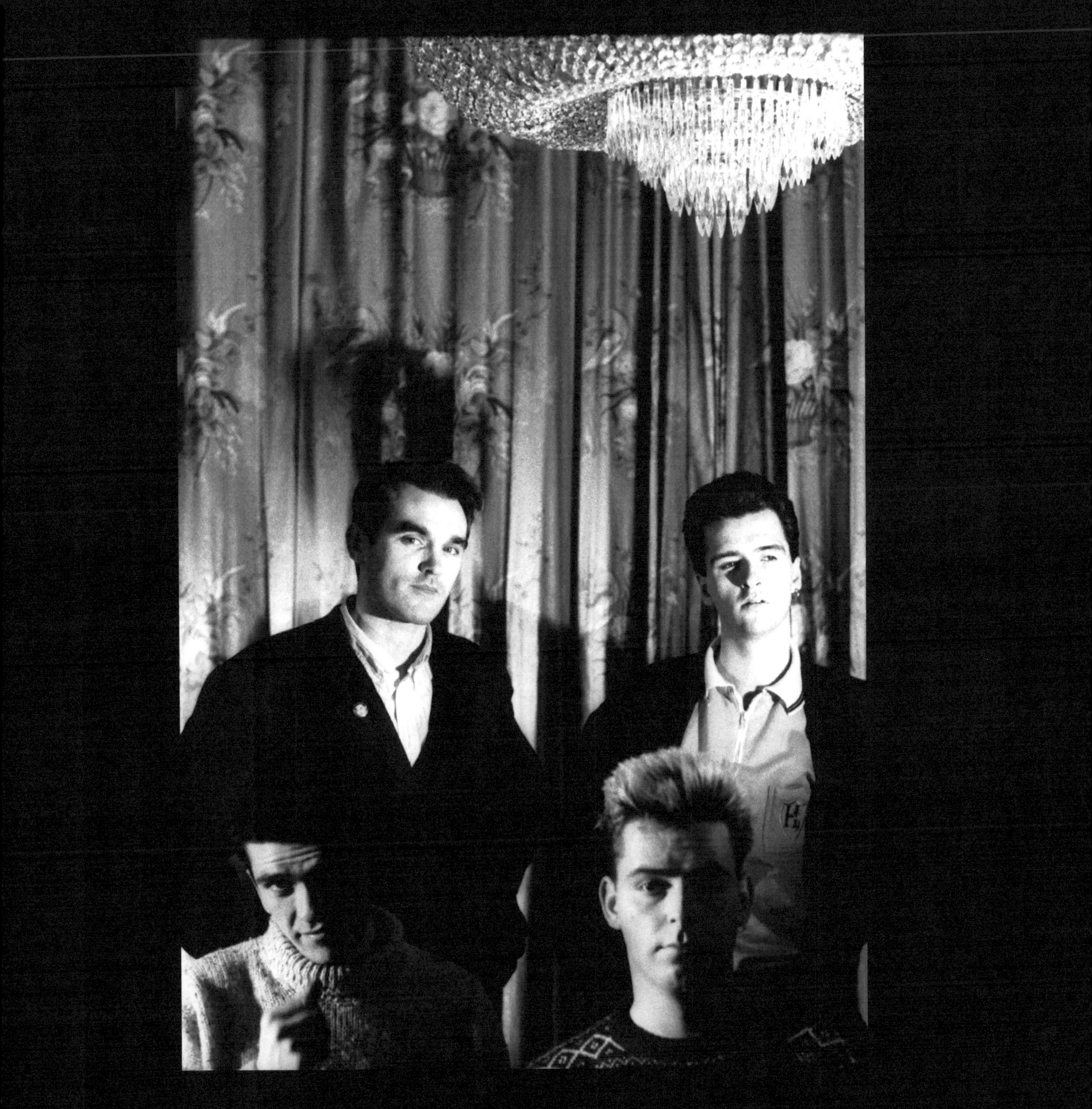

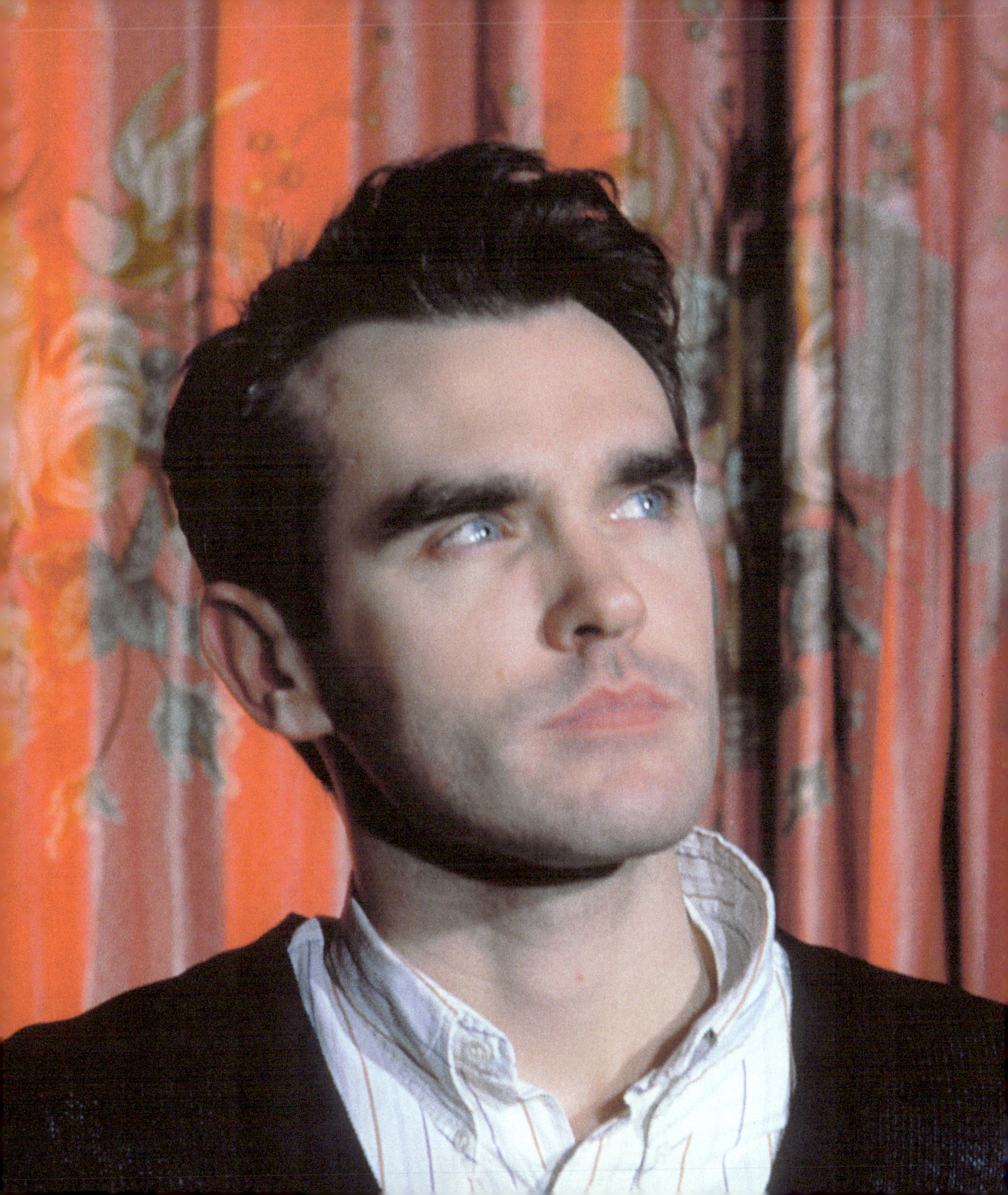

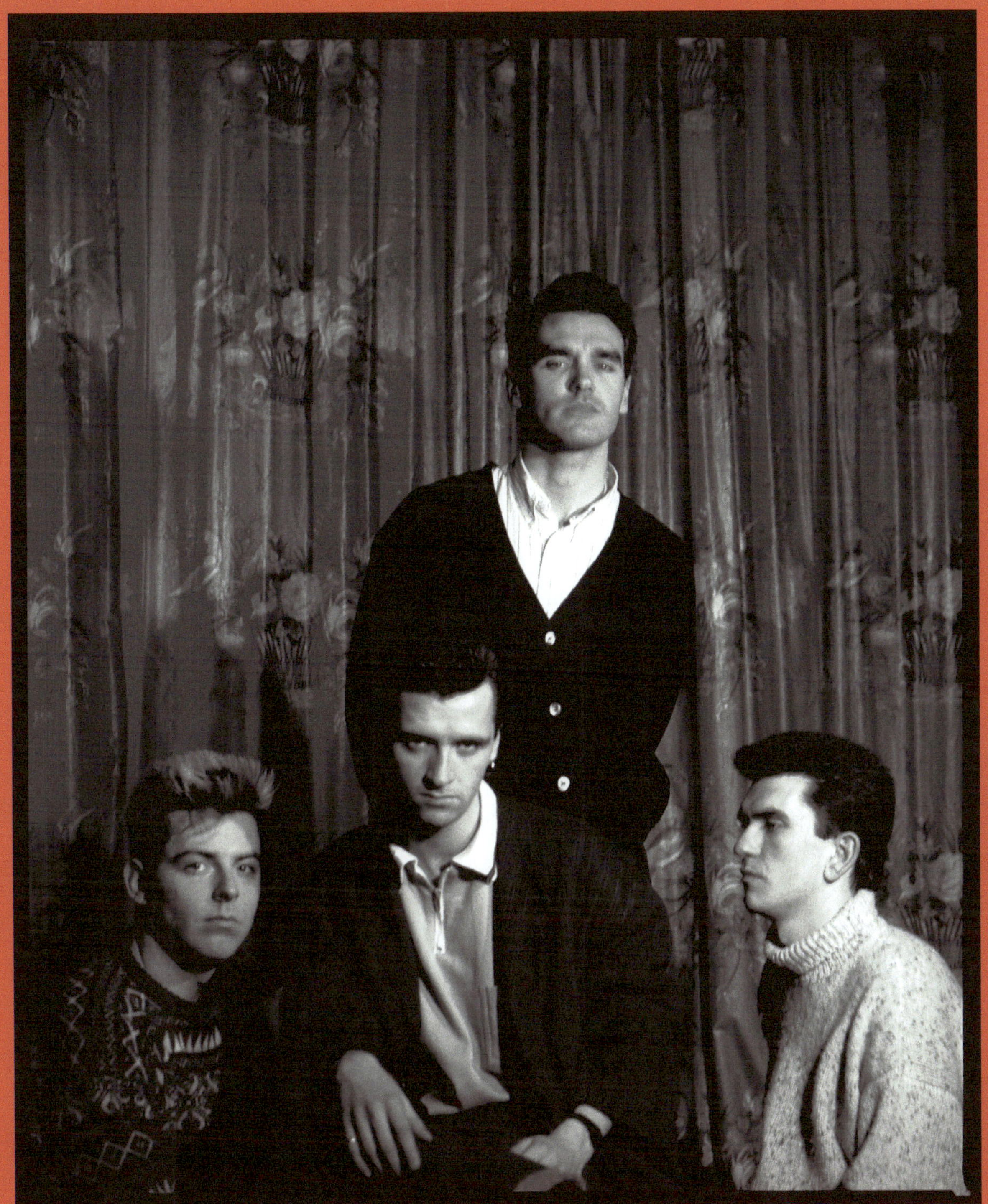

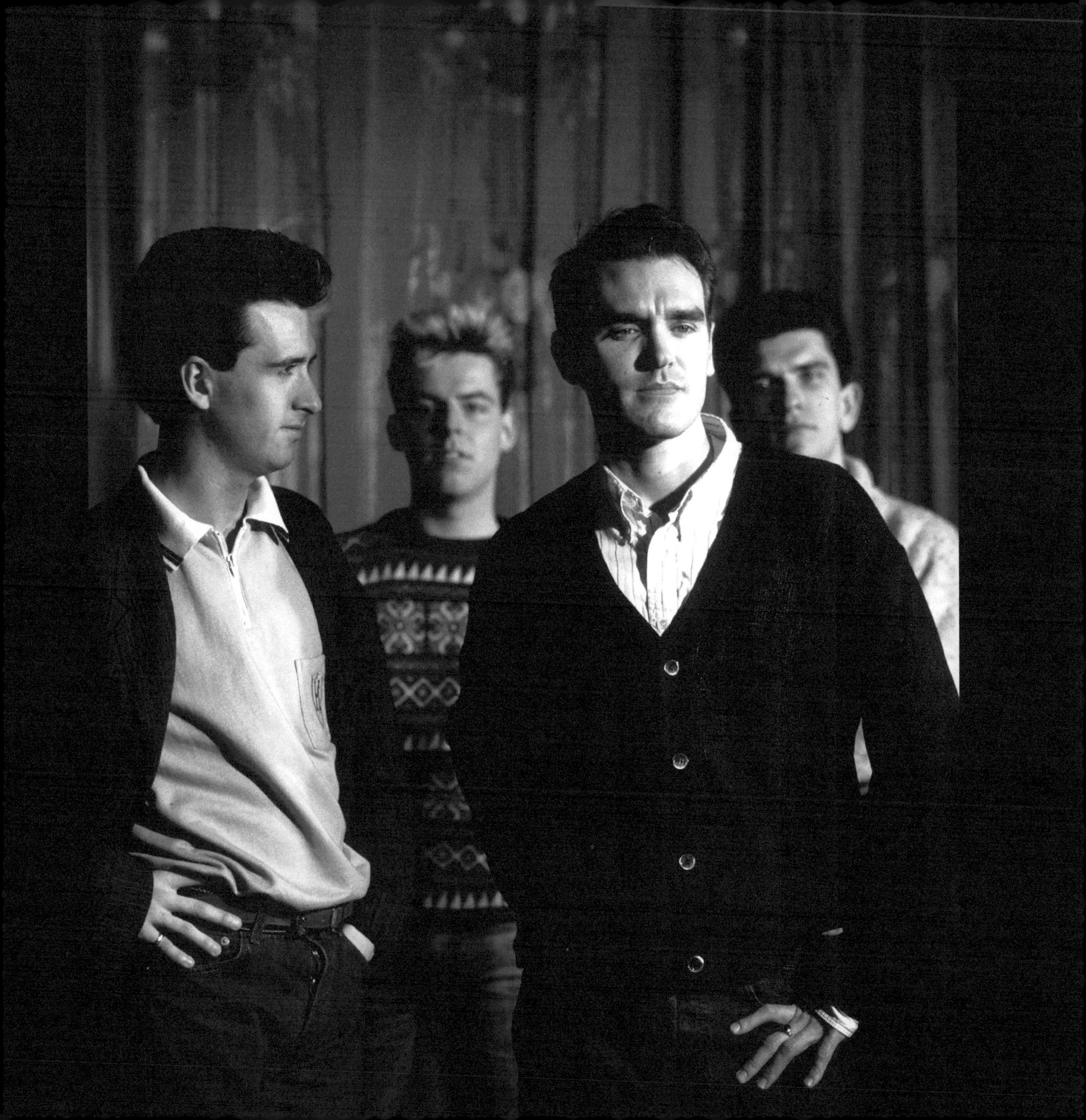

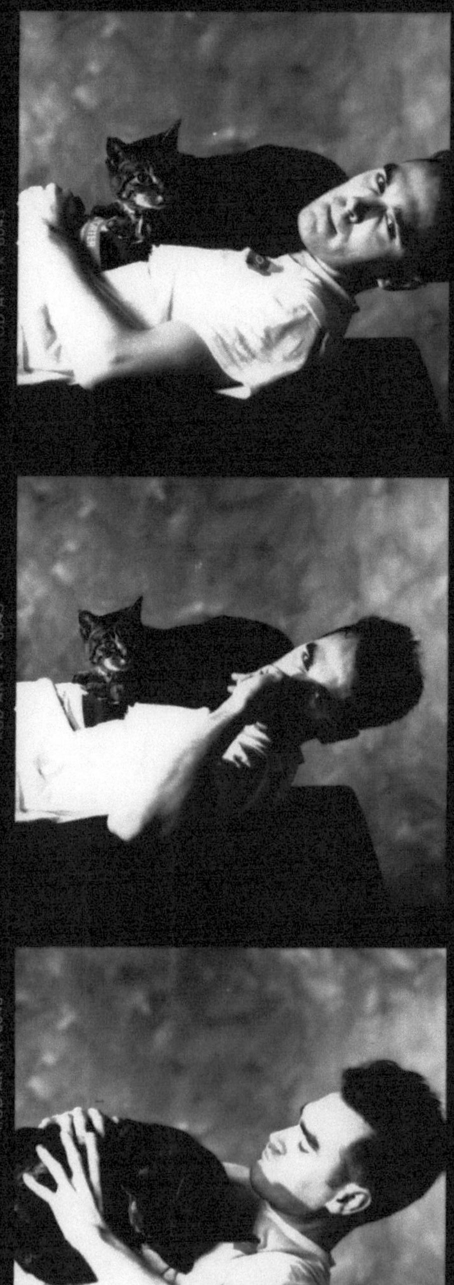

1989: Morrissey, solo, and his cat in London.

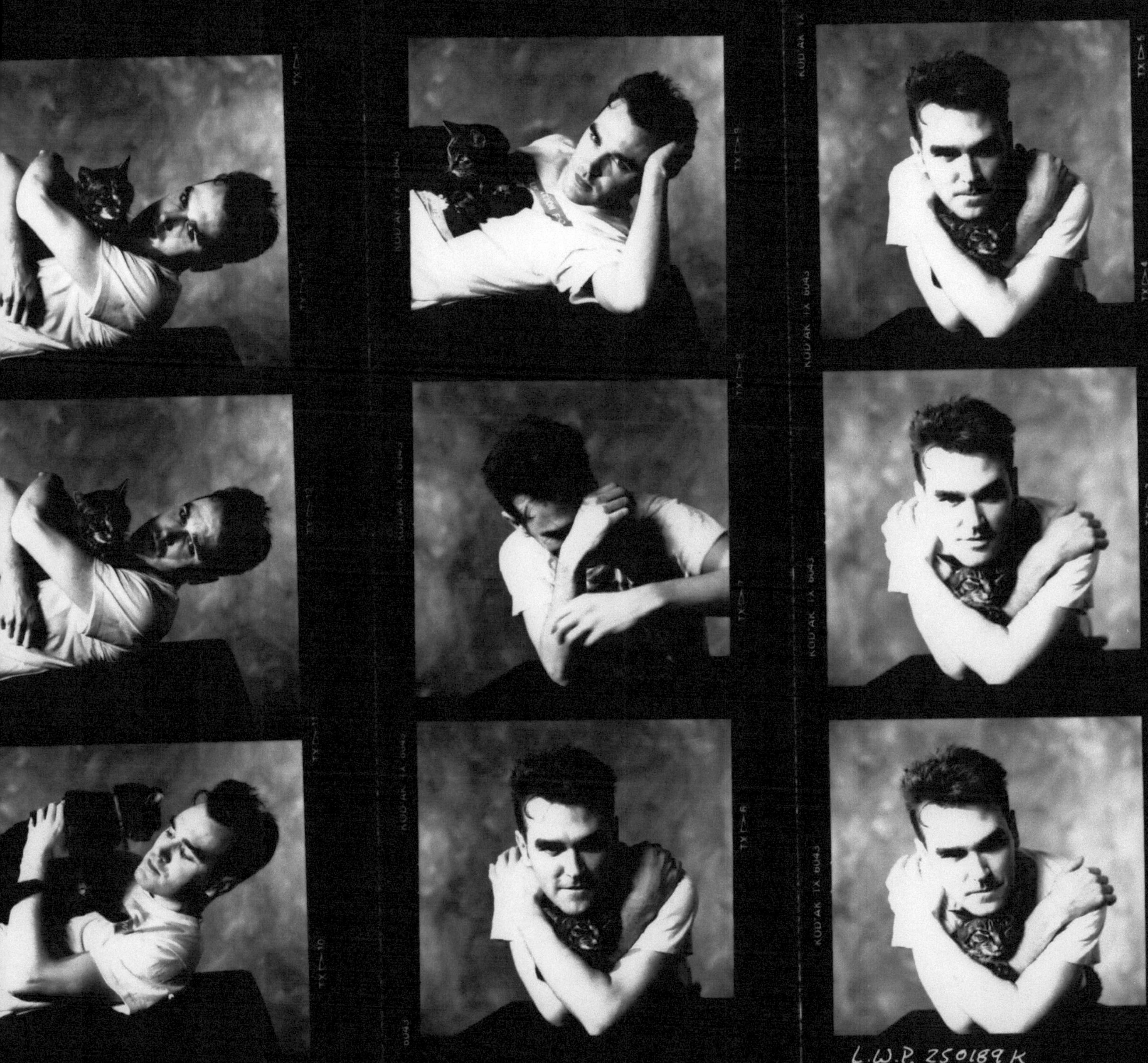
L.W.P. 250189 K

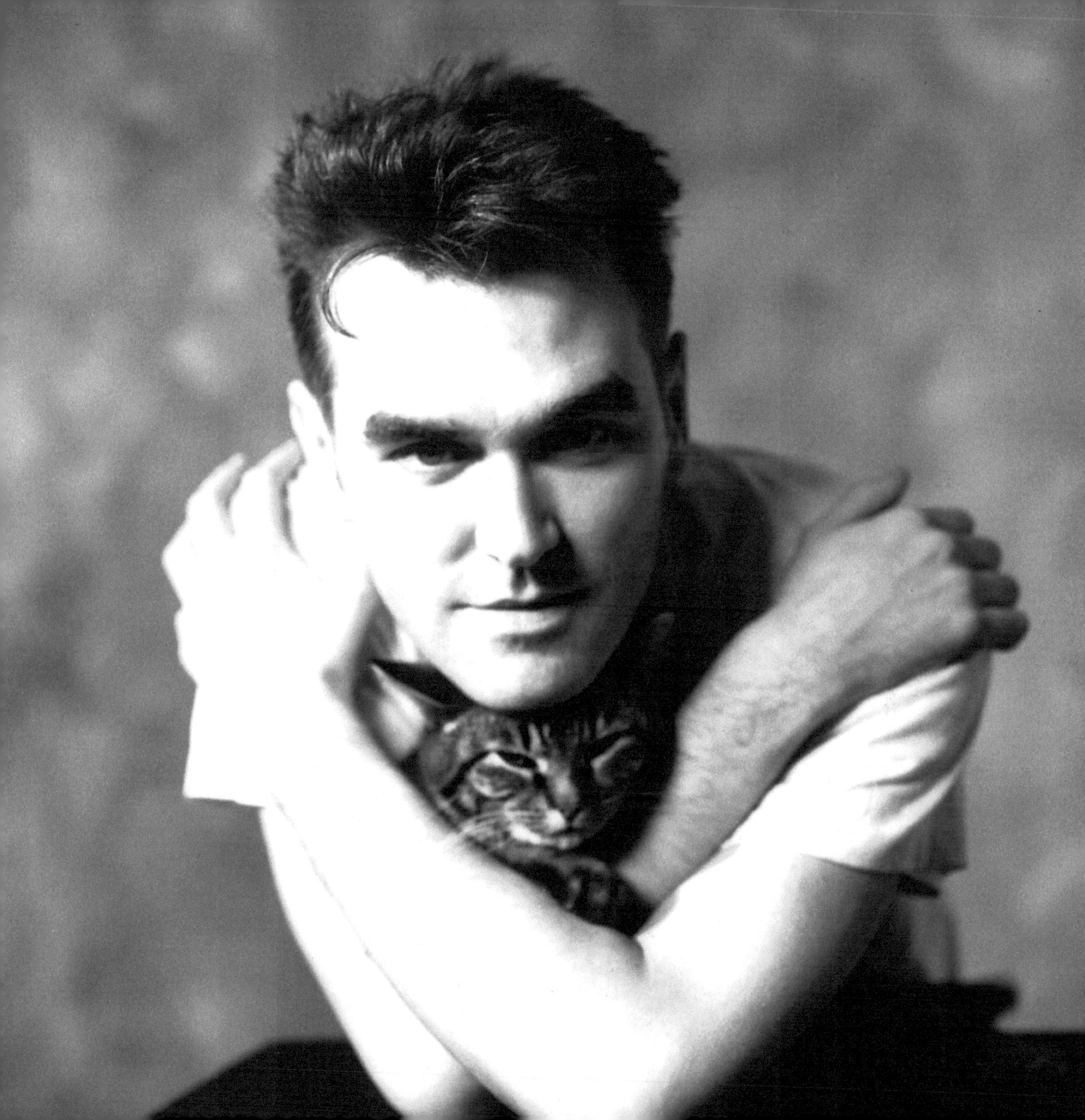

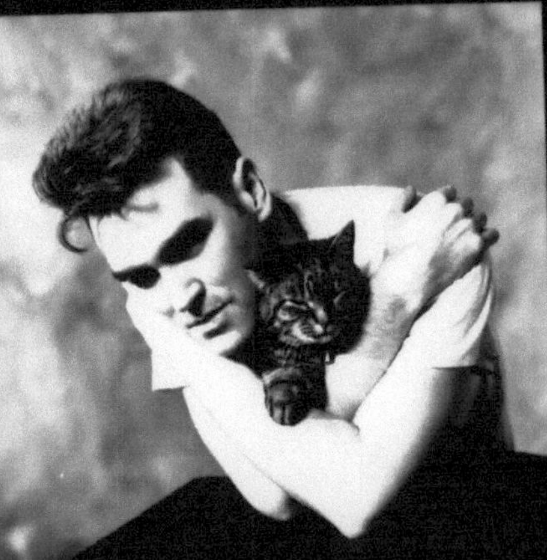

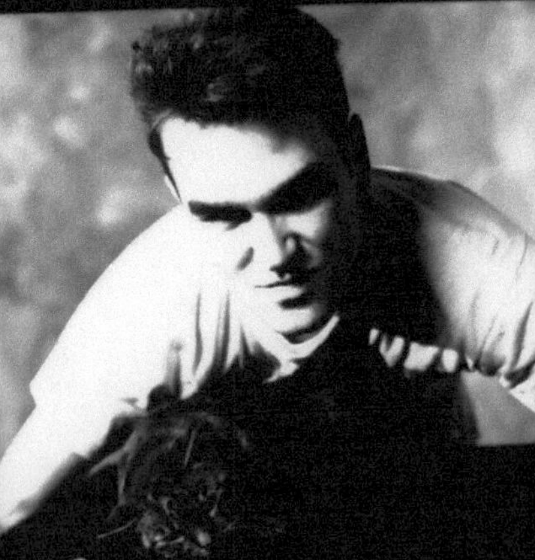

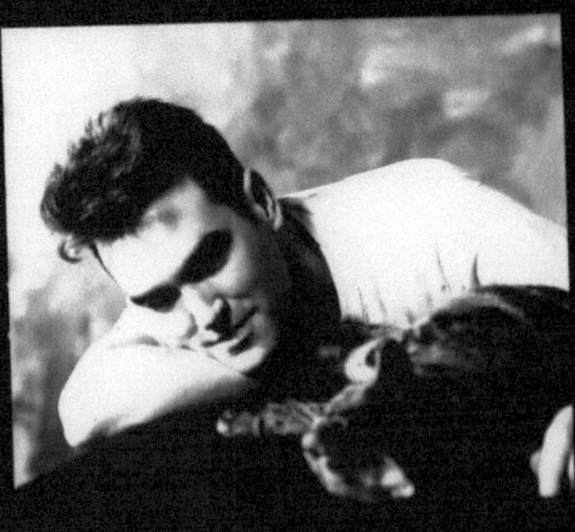

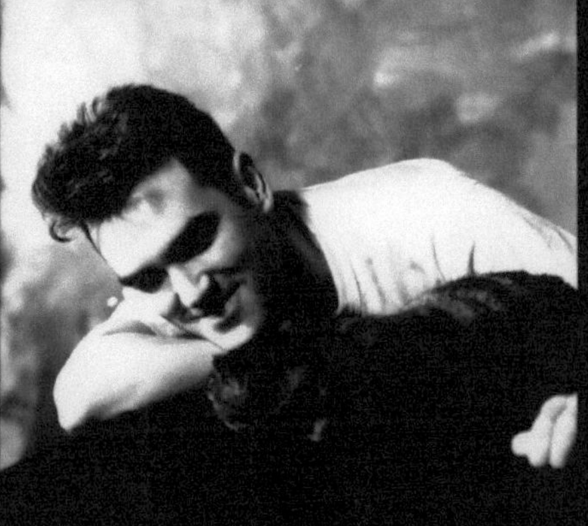

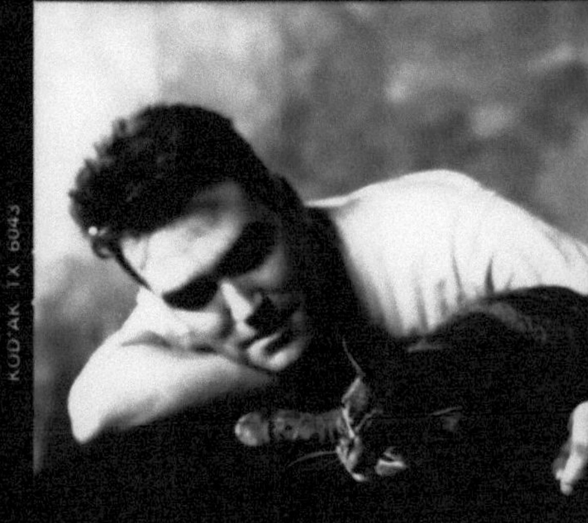

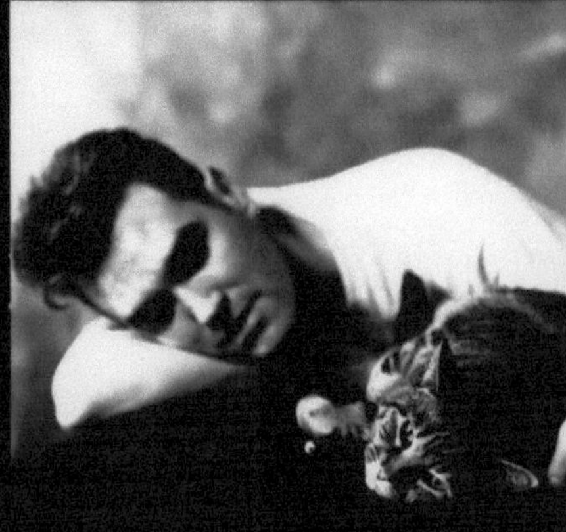

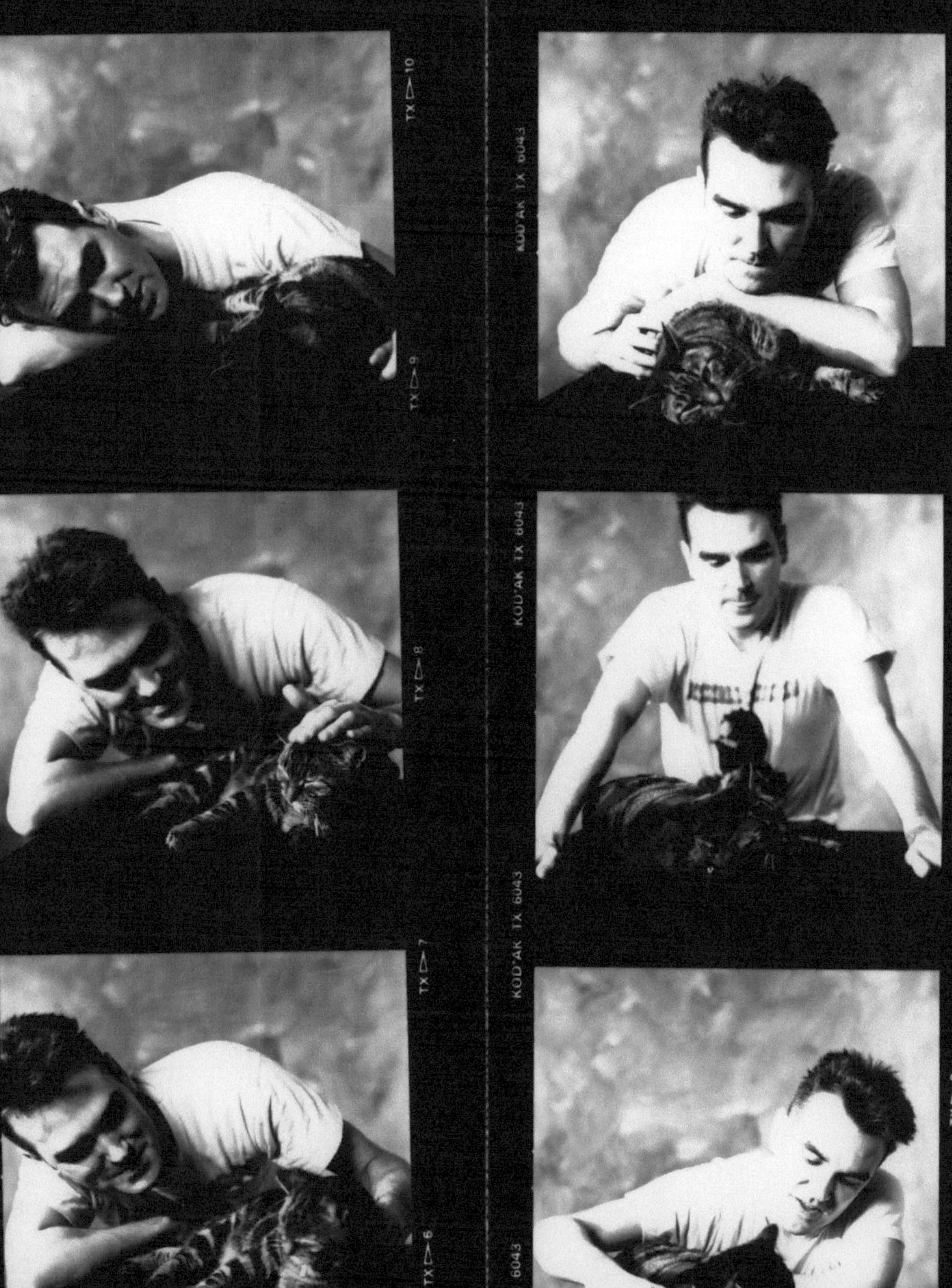

L.W.P. 250189G

46

Morrissey and pussy deep in thought.

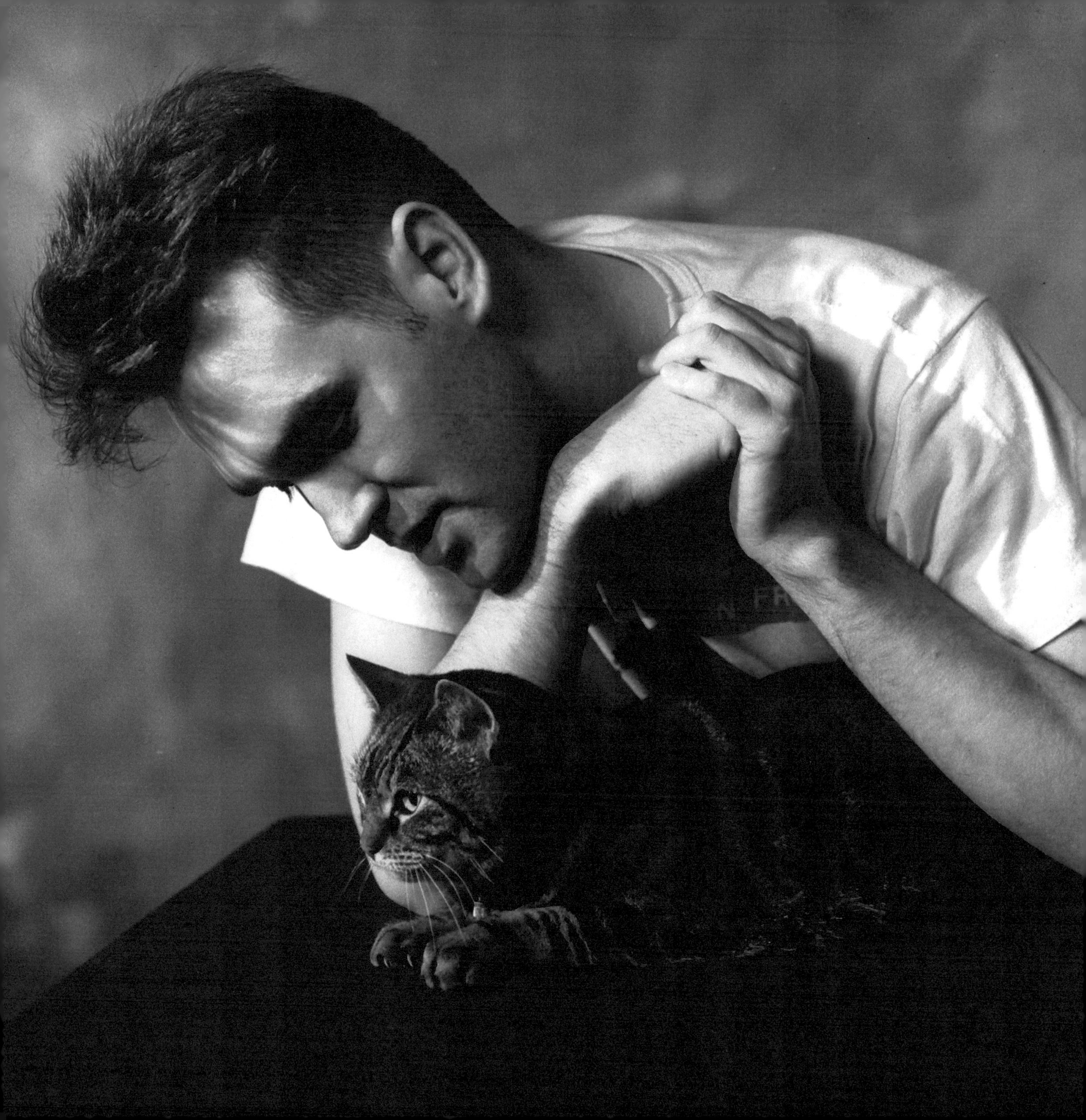

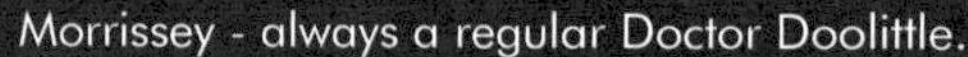

Morrissey - always a regular Doctor Doolittle.

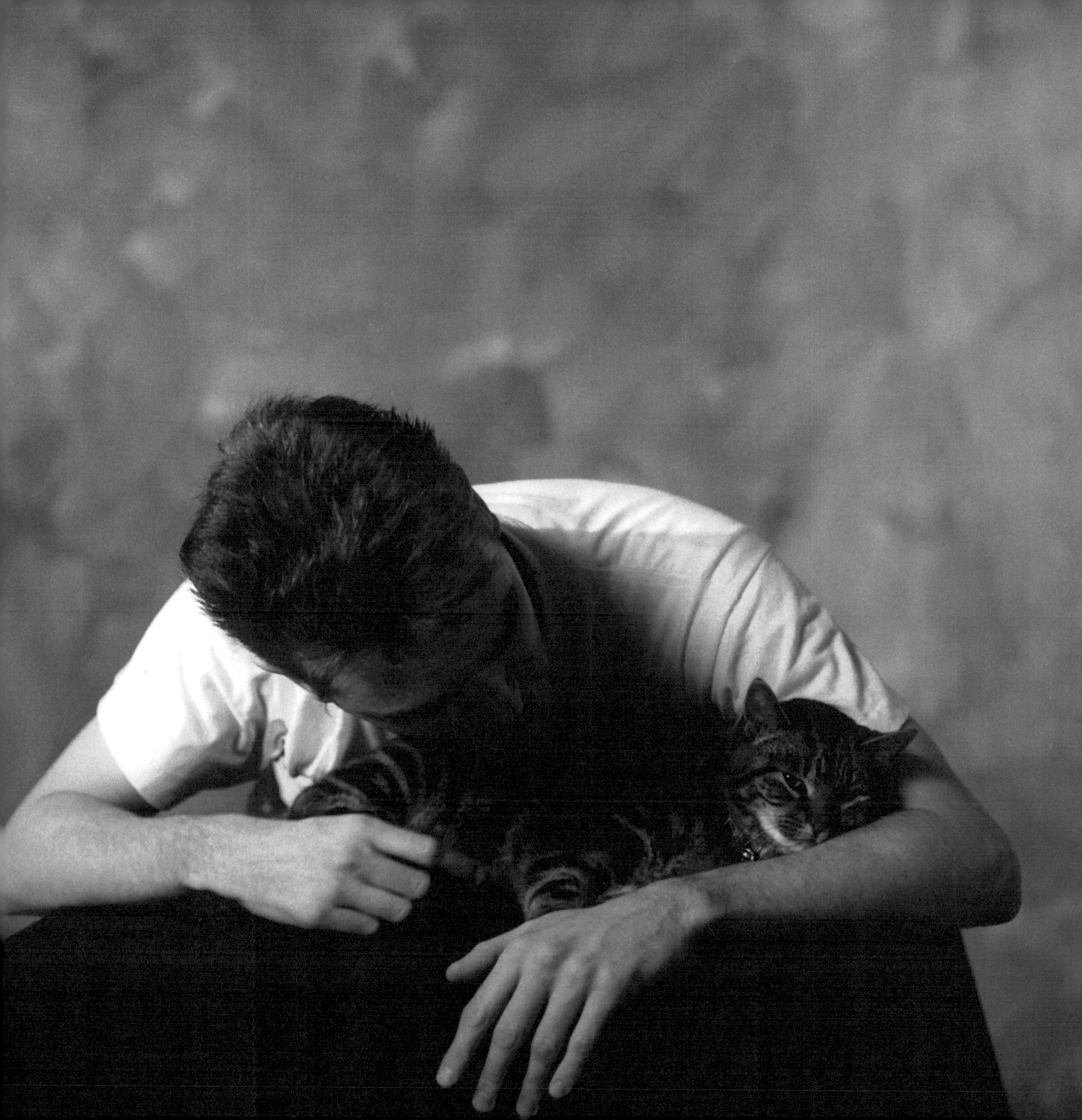

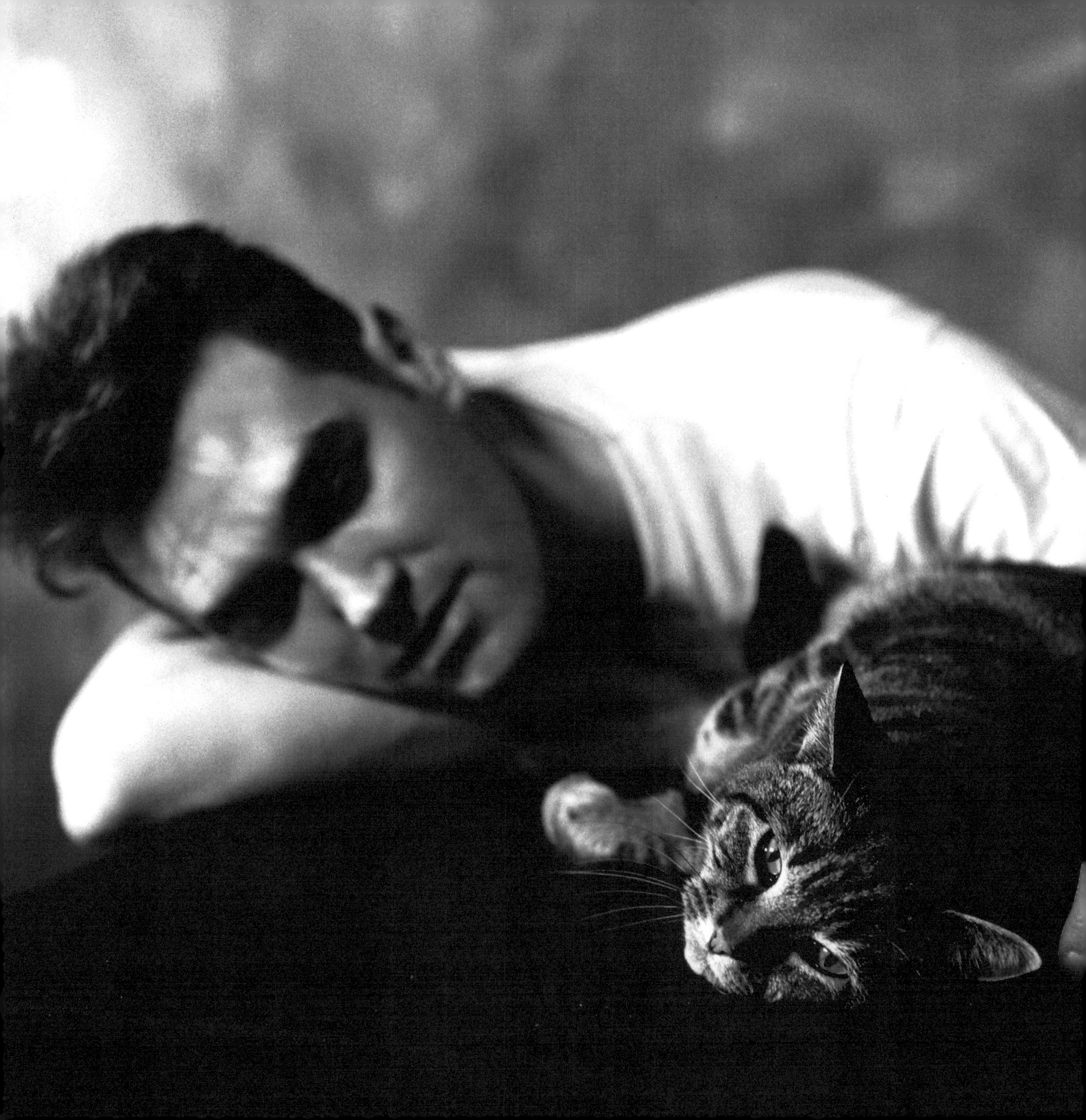

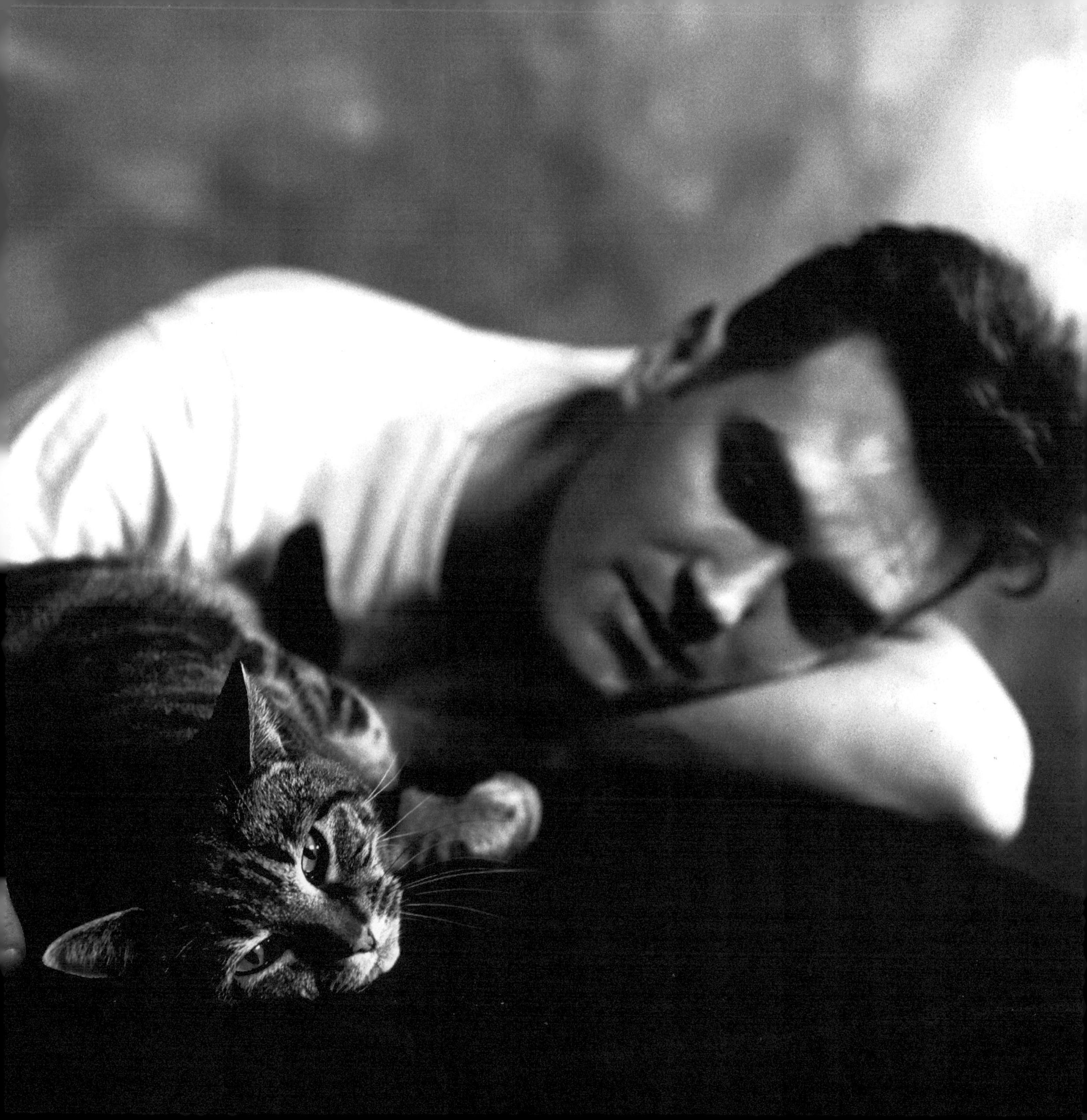

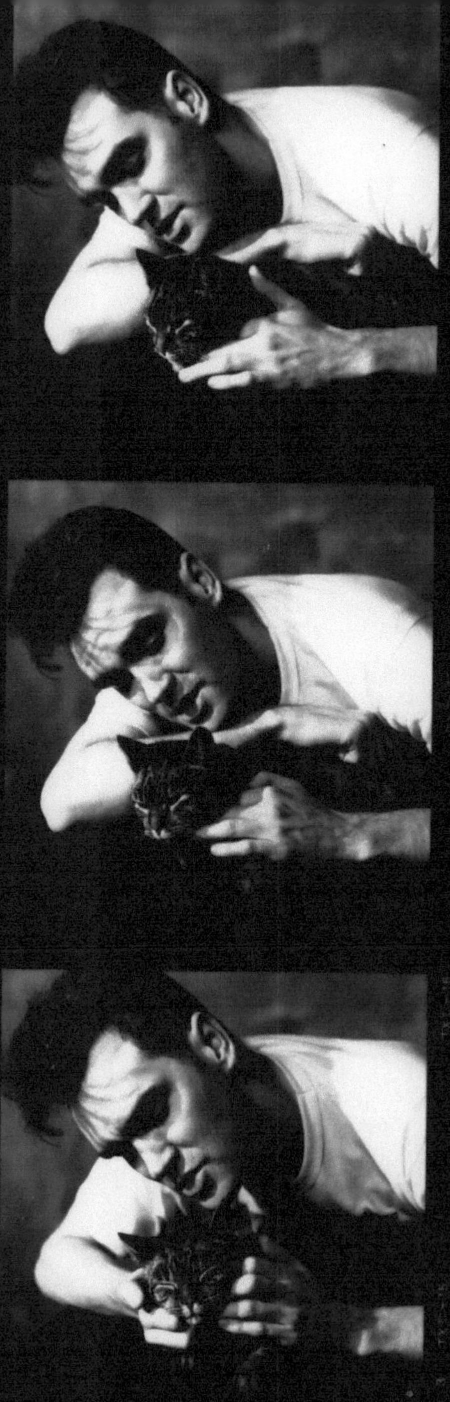

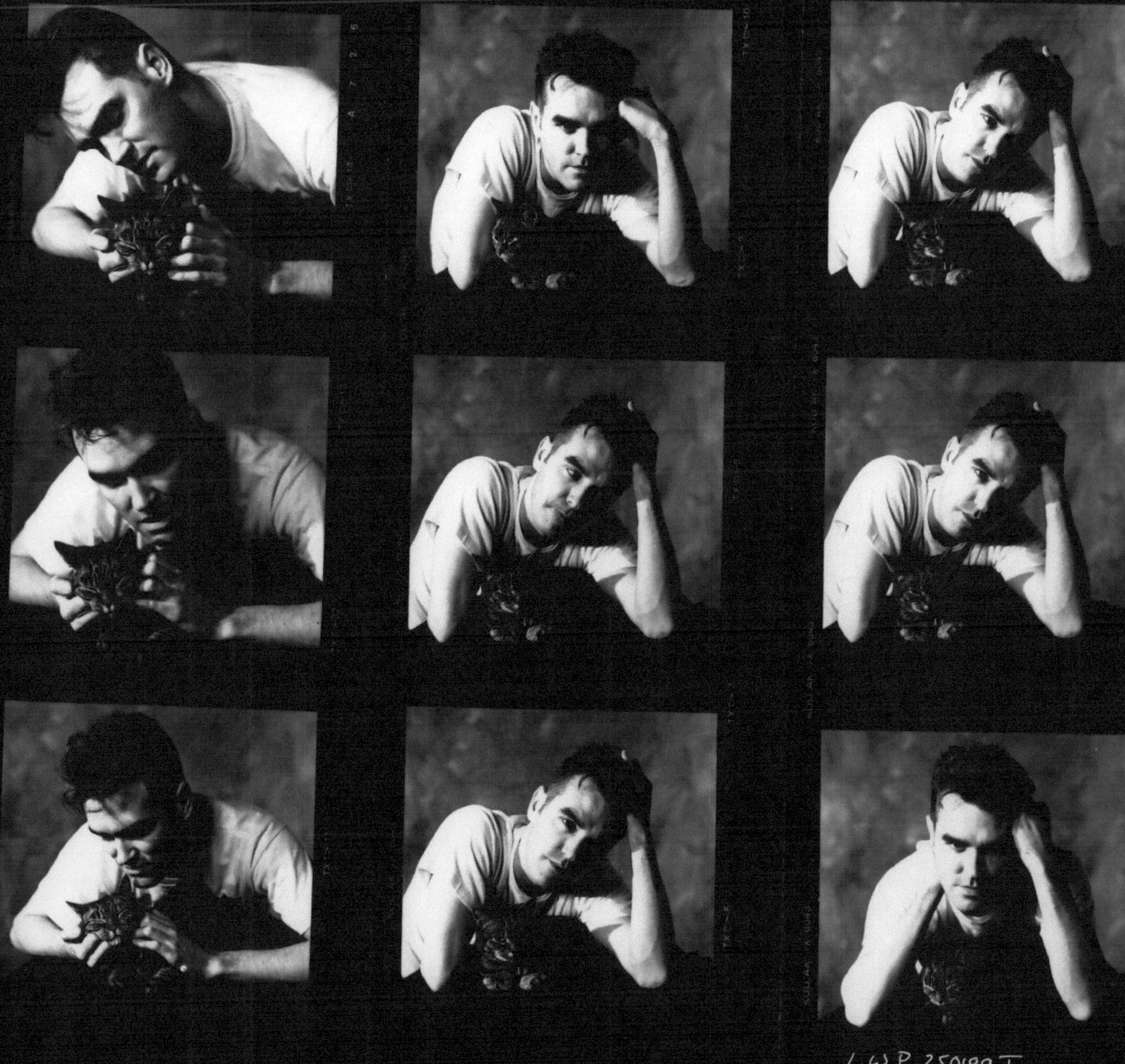
L.W.P. 250189 J

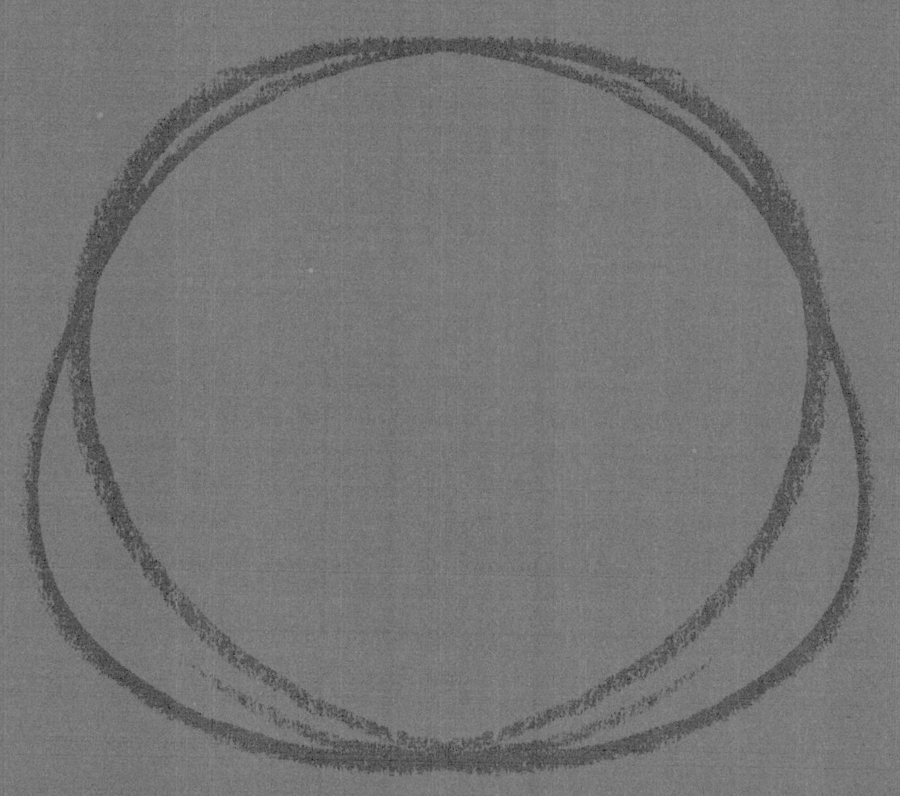

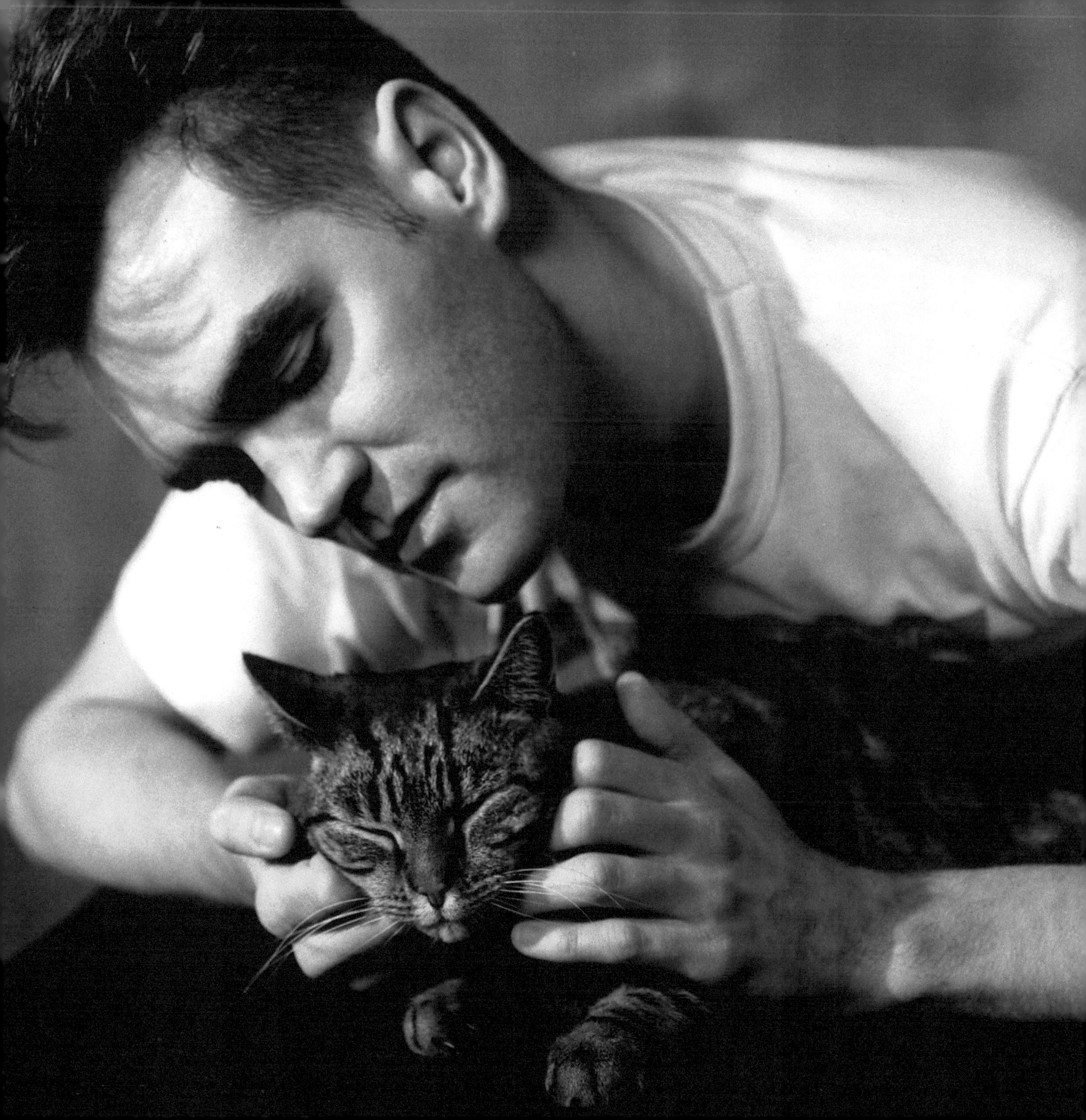

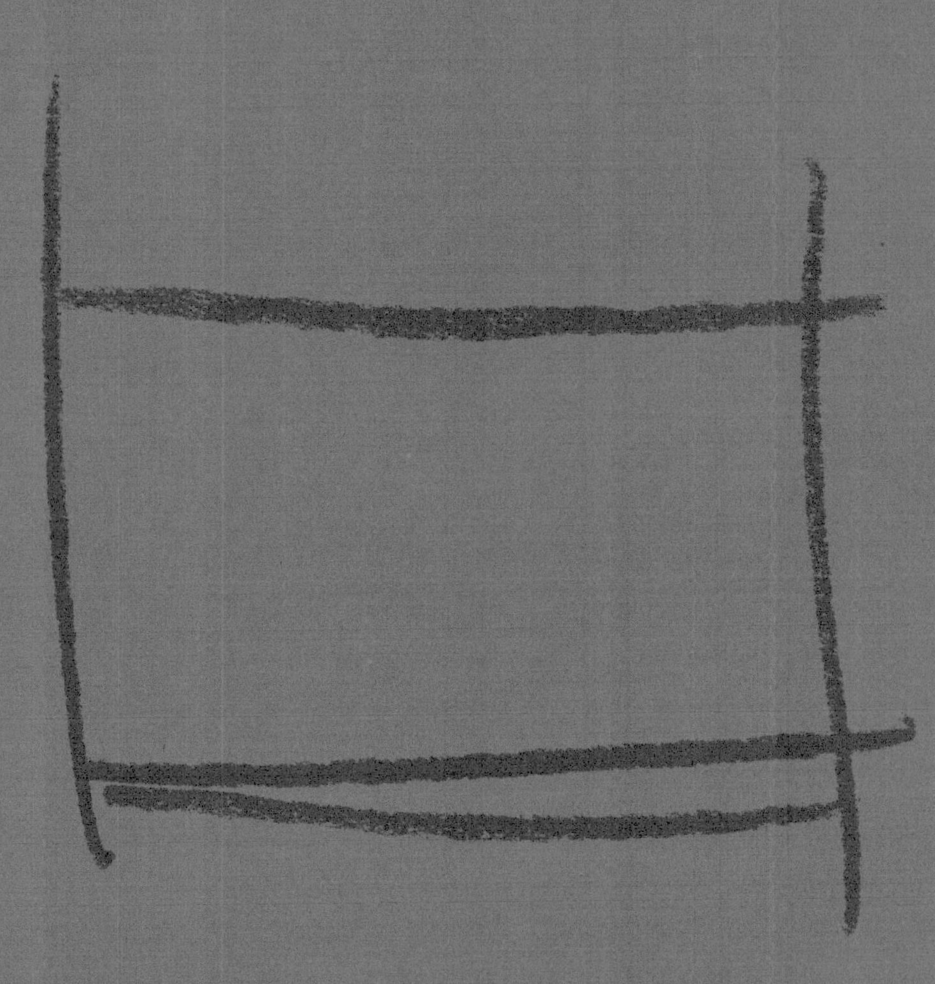

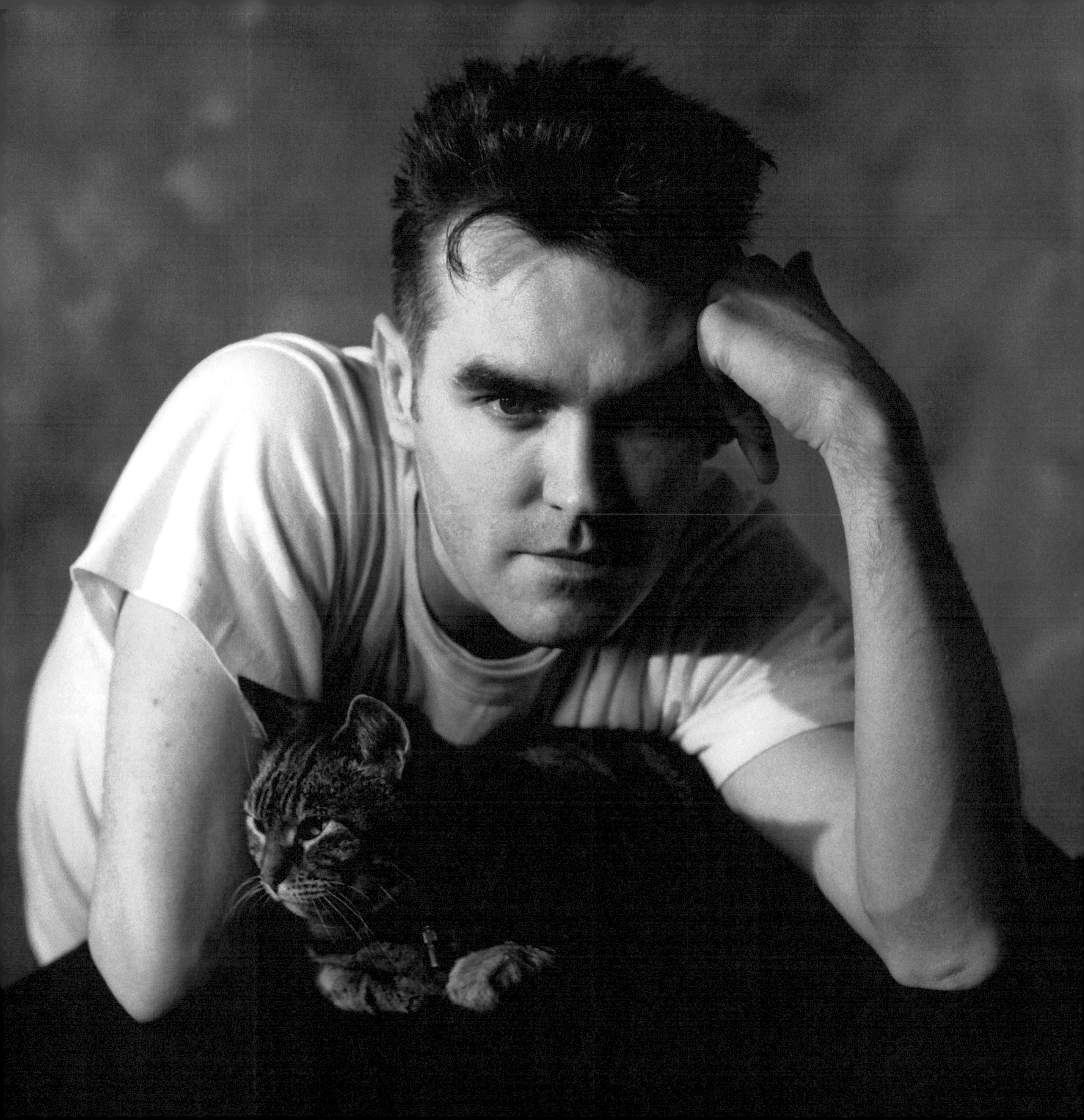

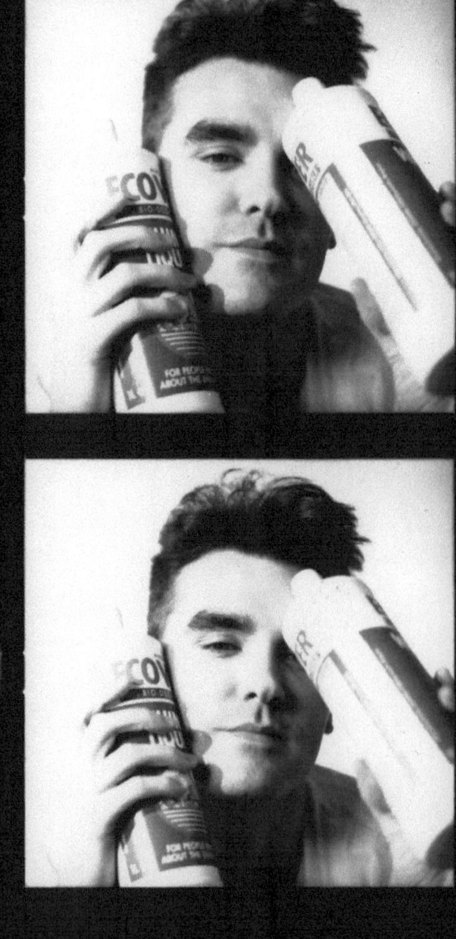

For hands that do dishes …

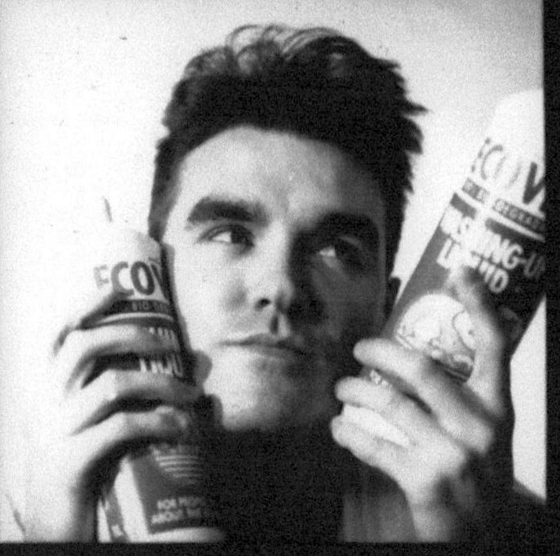

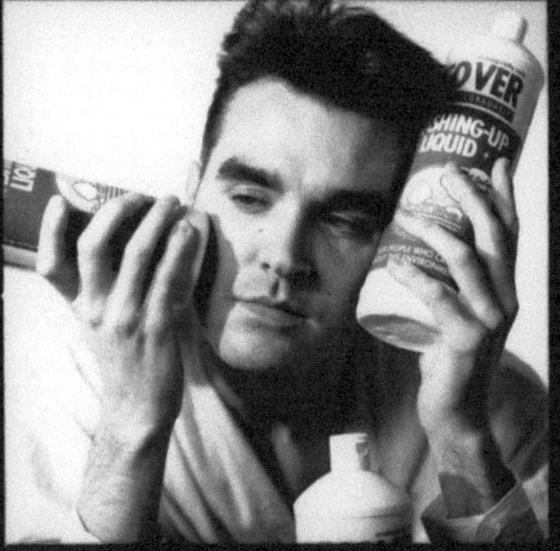

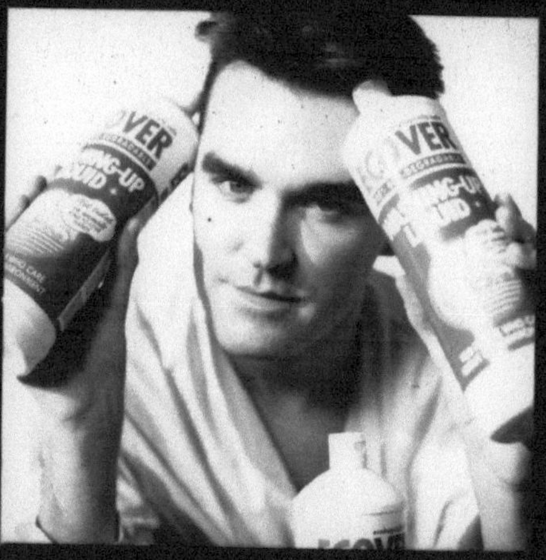

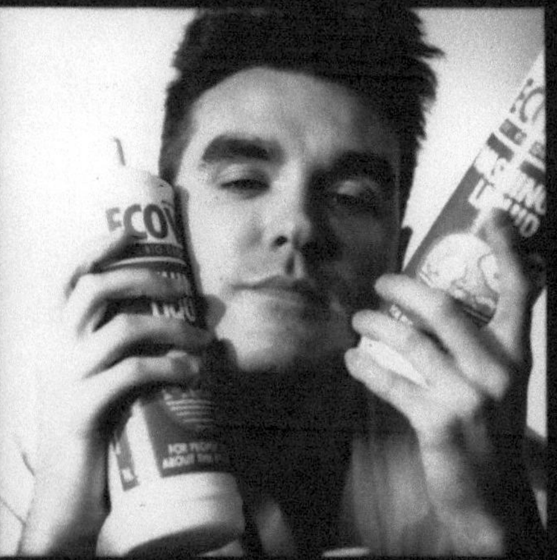

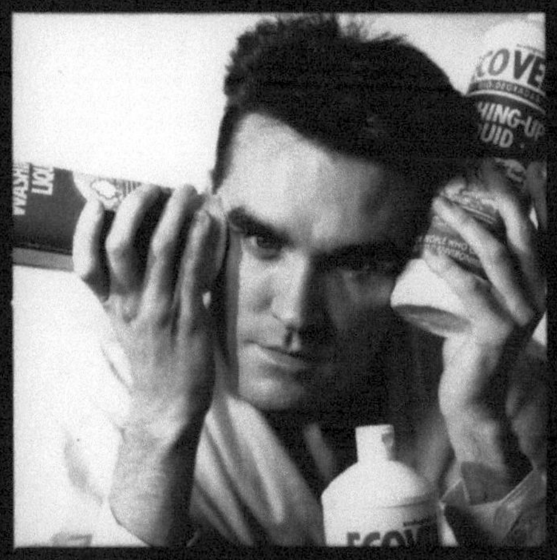

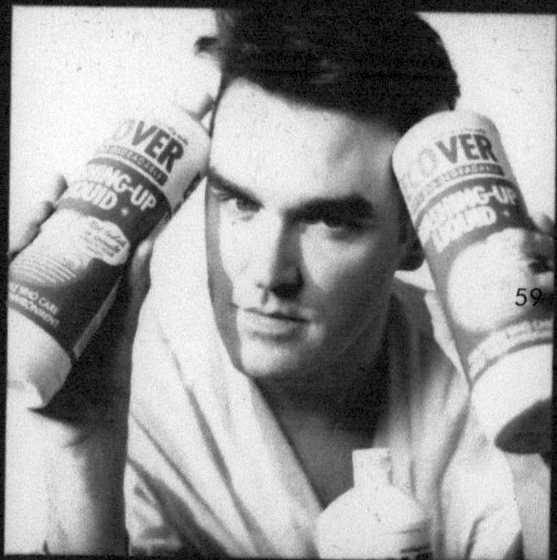

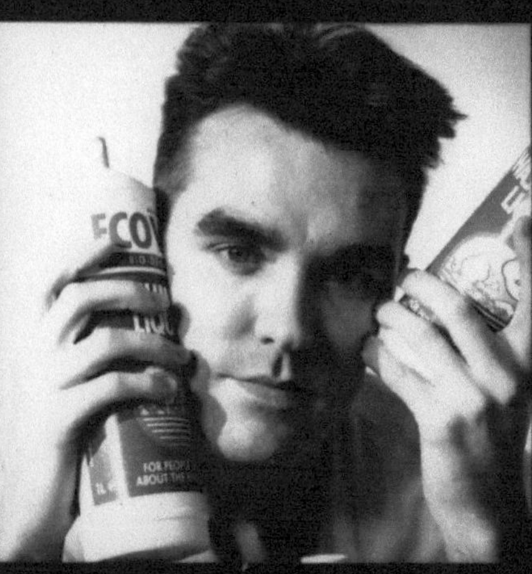

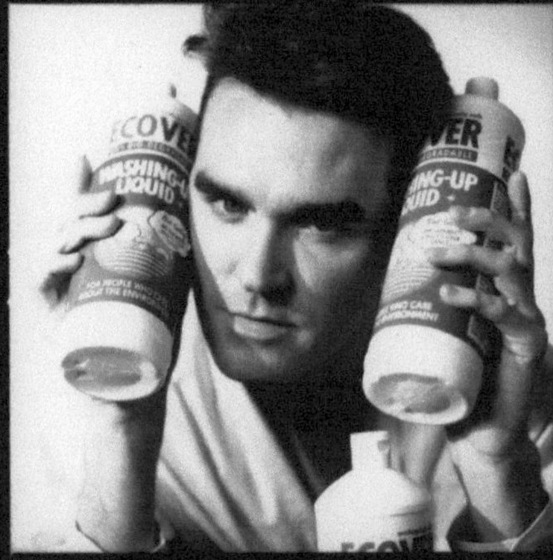

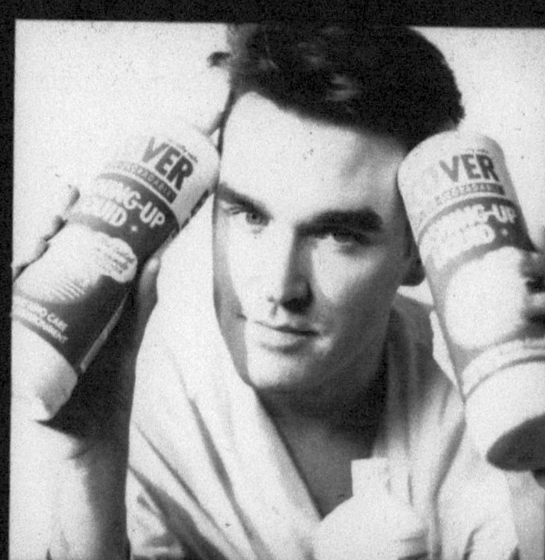

ECOVER
WASHING-UP
LIQUID

ECOVER
WASHING-UP
LIQUID

ECOVER
WASHING-UP
LIQUID

ECOVER

ECOVER
WASHING-UP
LIQUID

ECOVER
WASHING-UP
LIQUID

ECOVER
LIQUID

ECOVER
WASHING-UP
LIQUID

ECOVER
WASHING-UP
LIQUID

L.W.P. 250189 M

Kitchen sink drama …

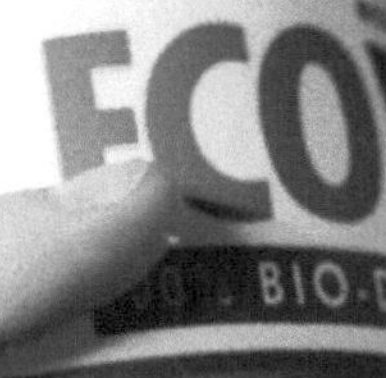

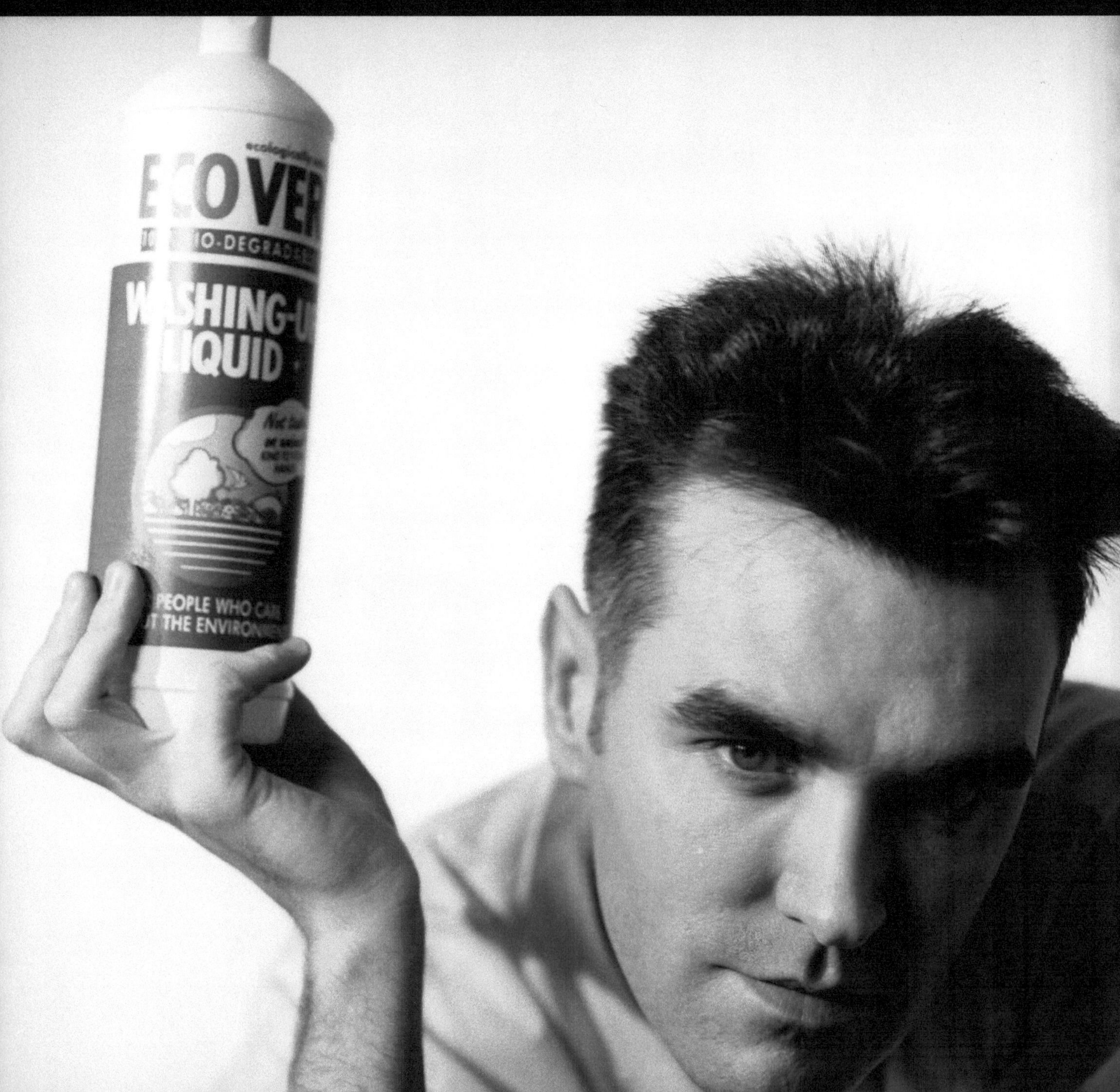
ECOVE
WASHING-U
LIQUID
PEOPLE WHO CA
THE ENVIRON

Forever green.

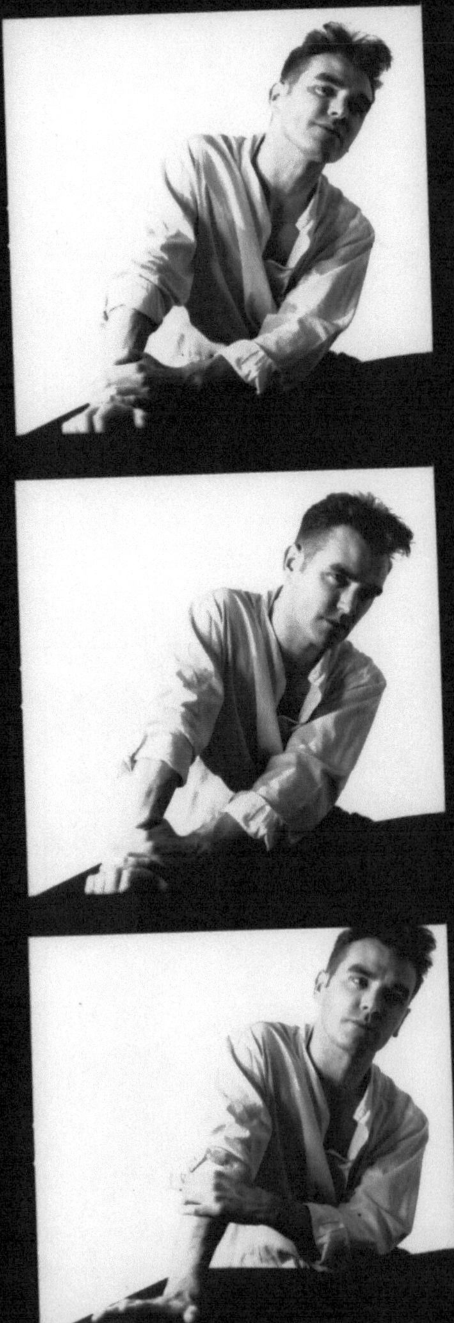

The camera loves him.

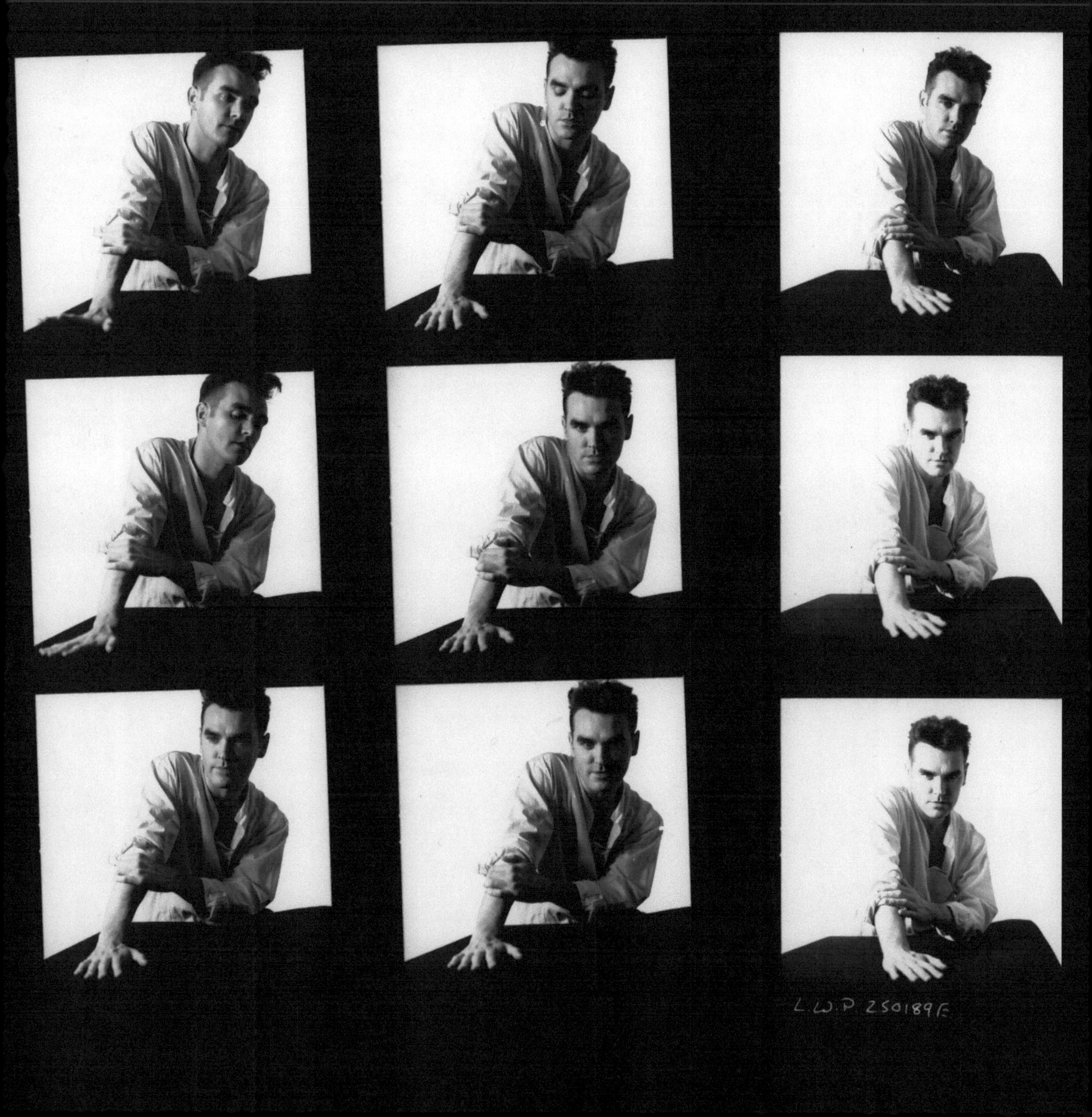

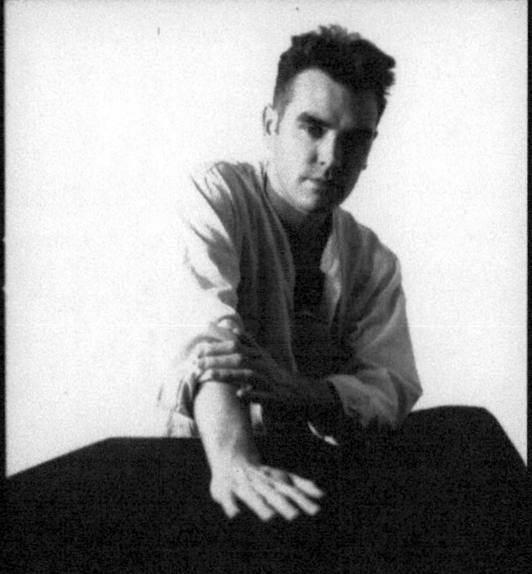

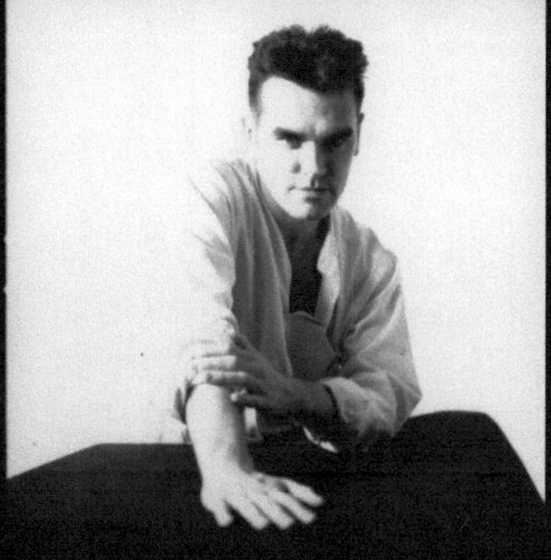

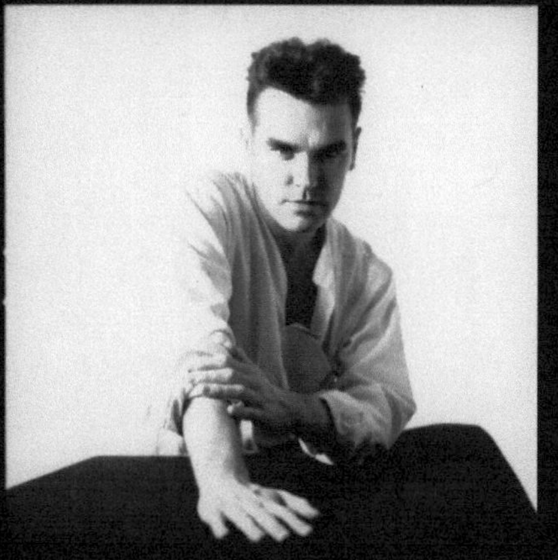

L.W.P 250189E

Morrissey, London, 1989.

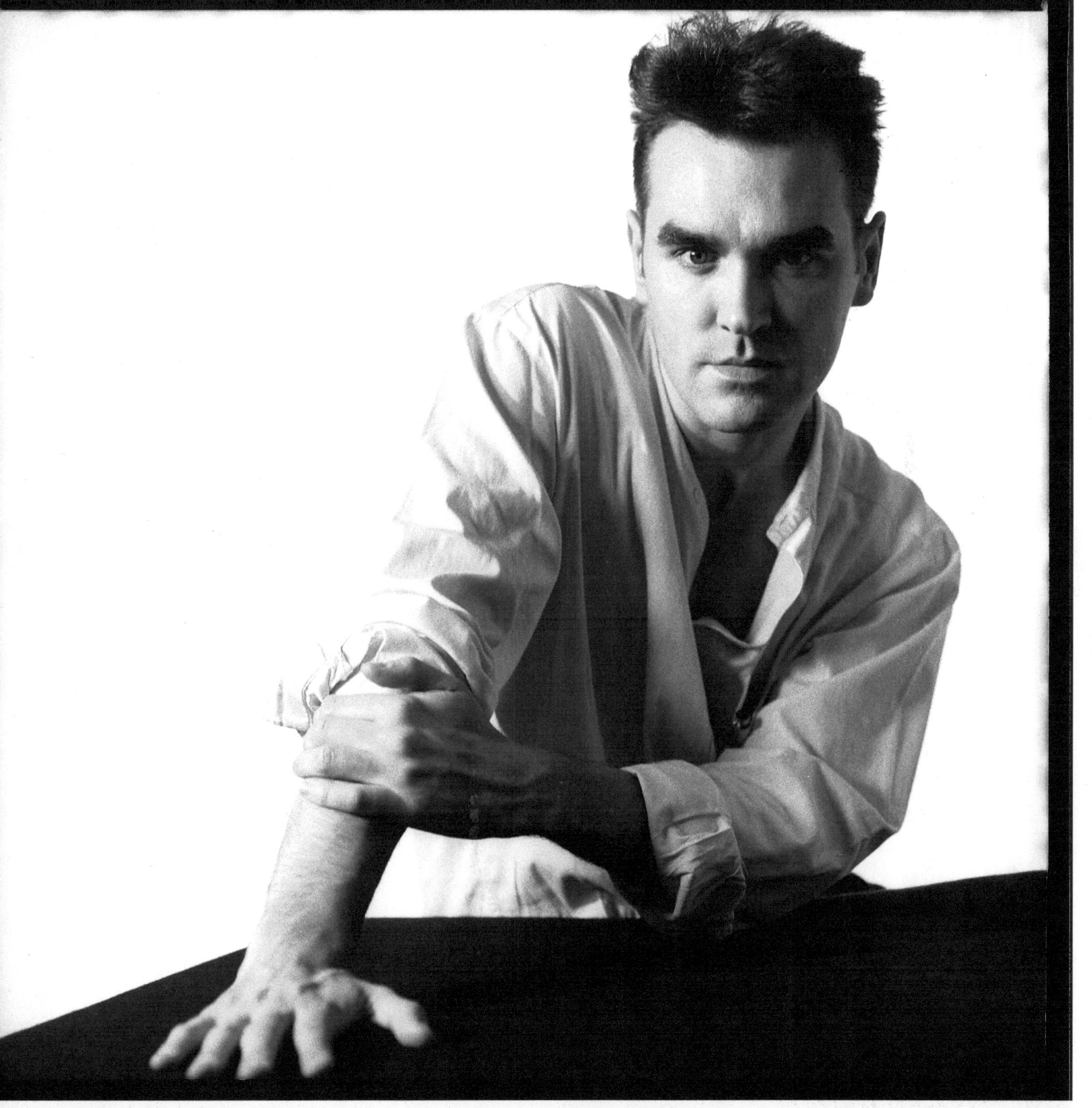

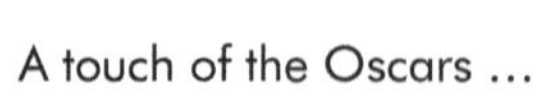

A touch of the Oscars …

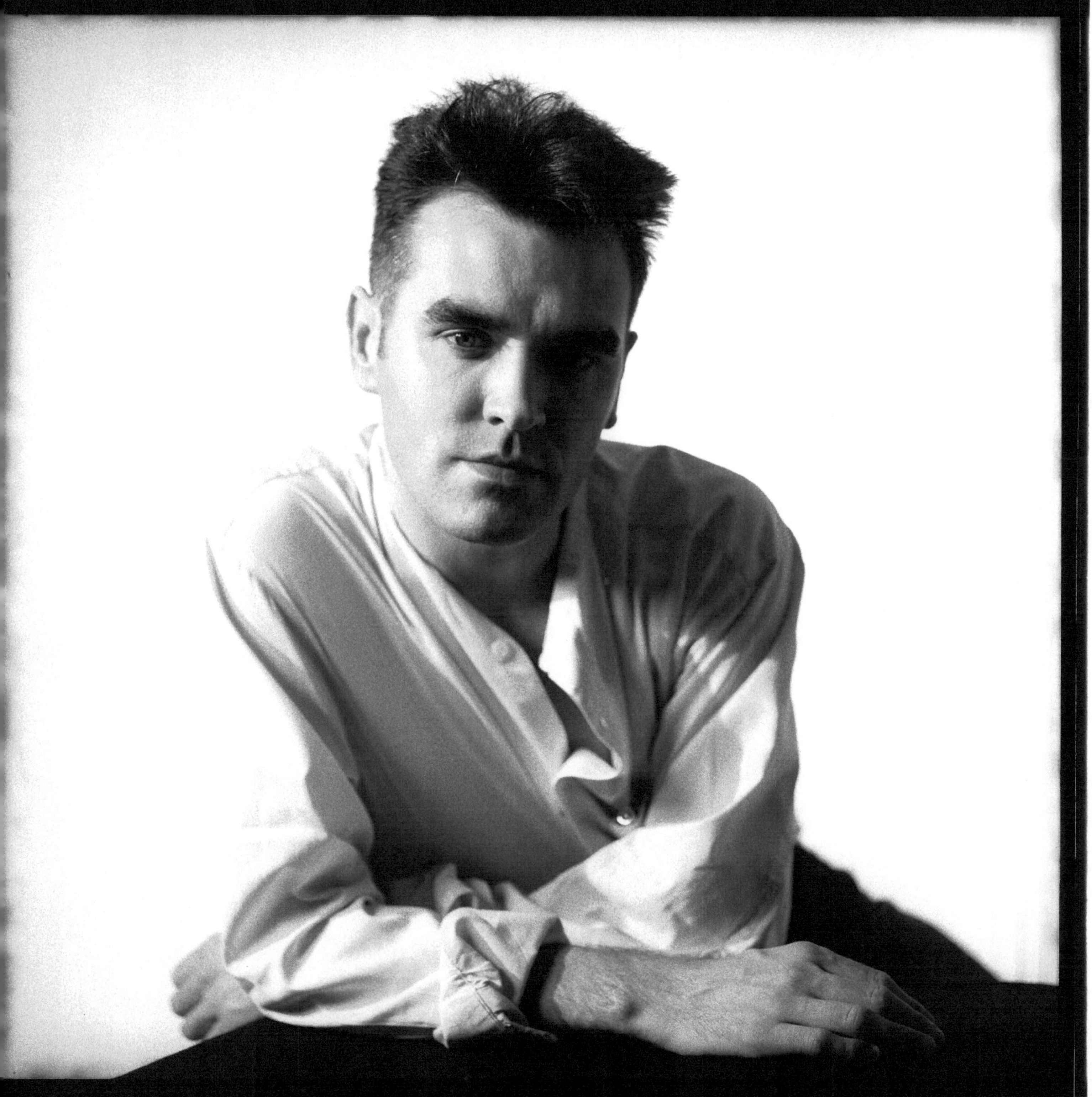

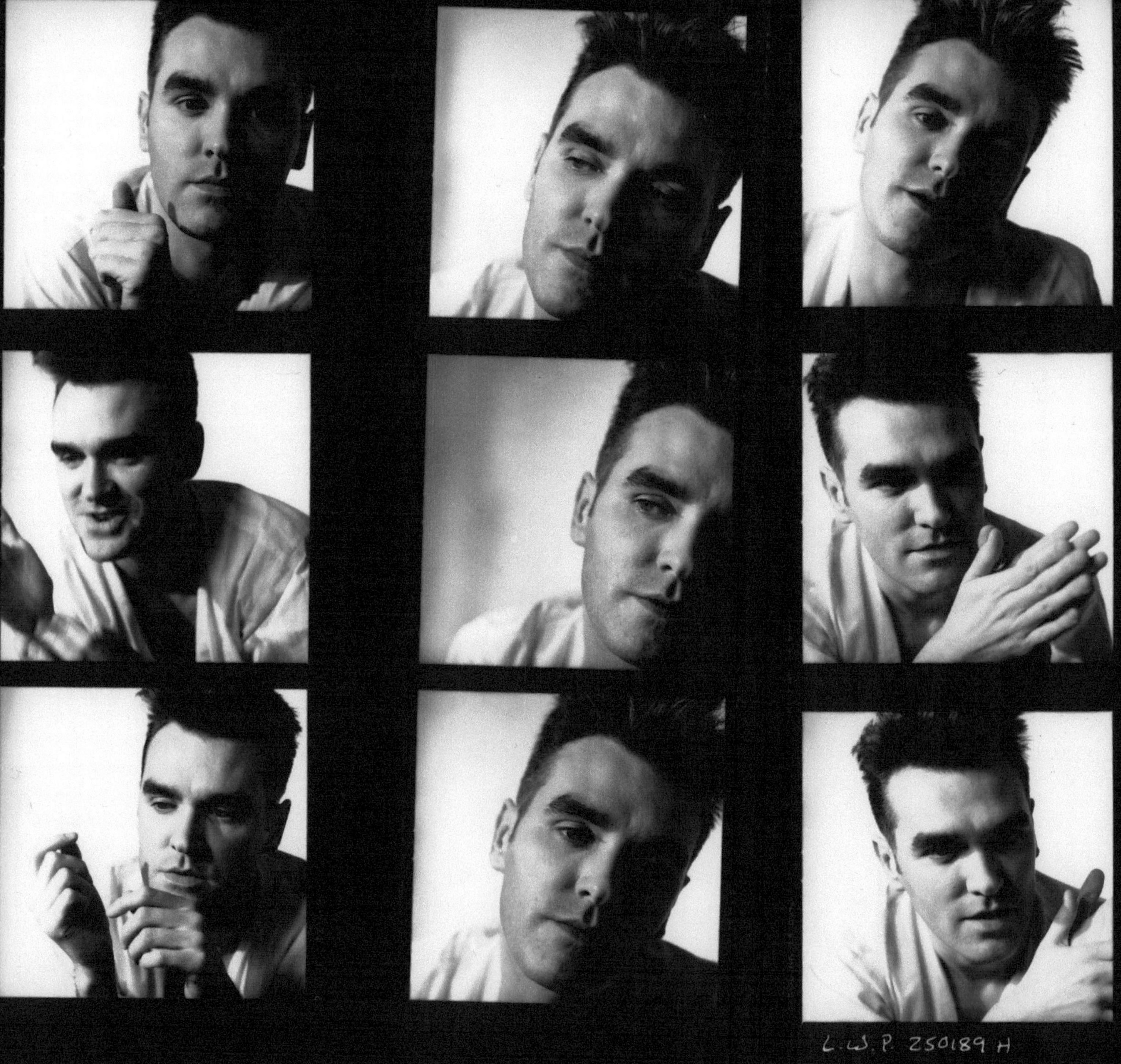
L.W.P. 250189 H

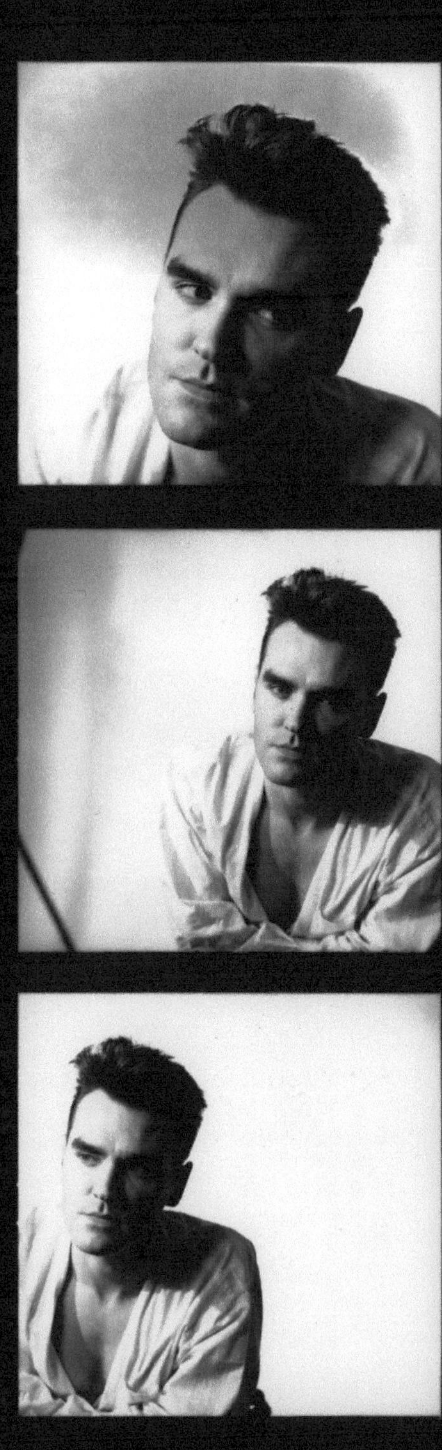

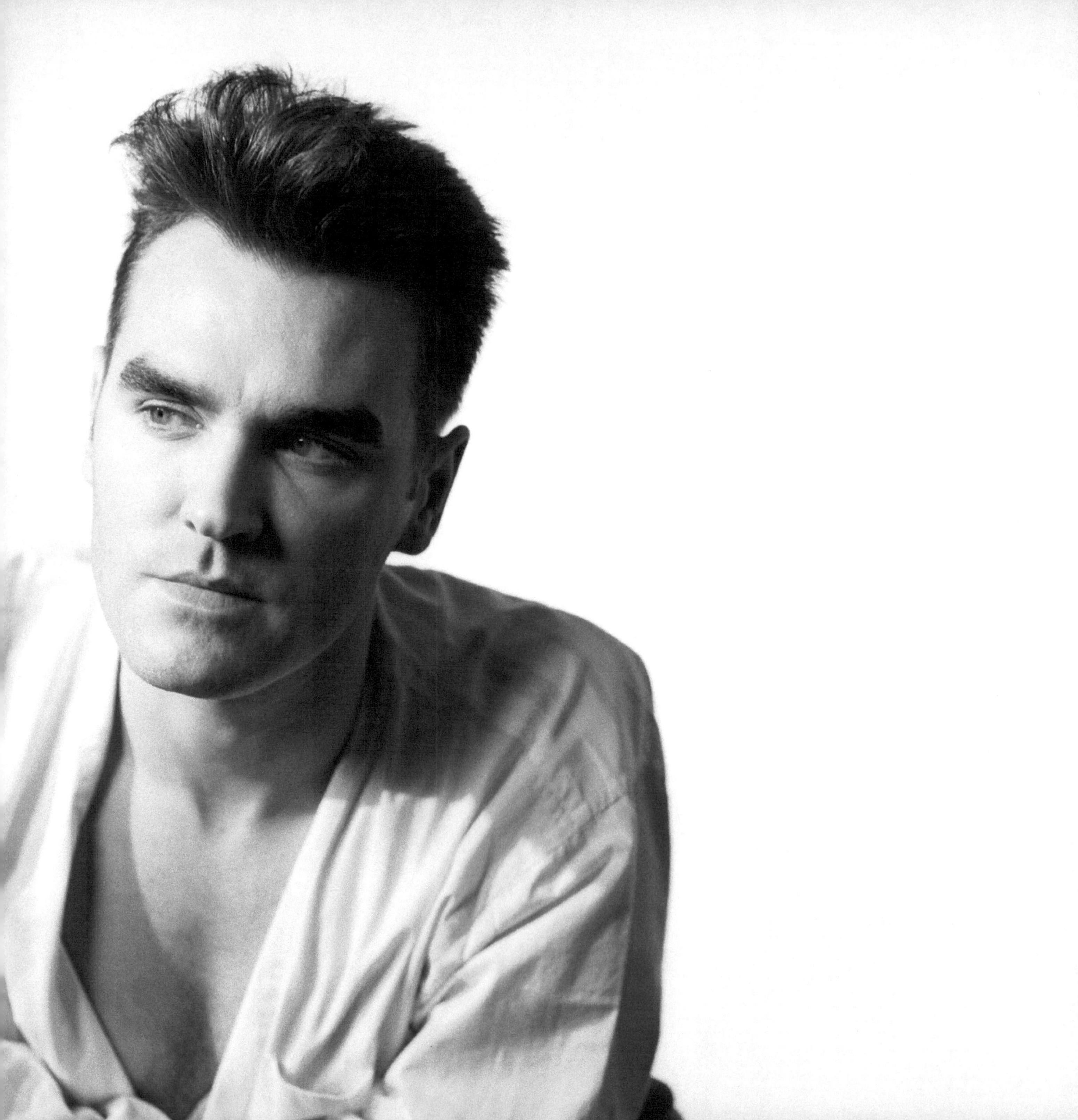

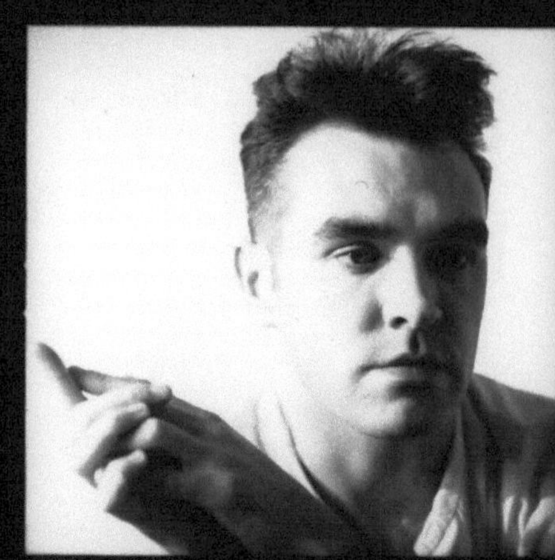

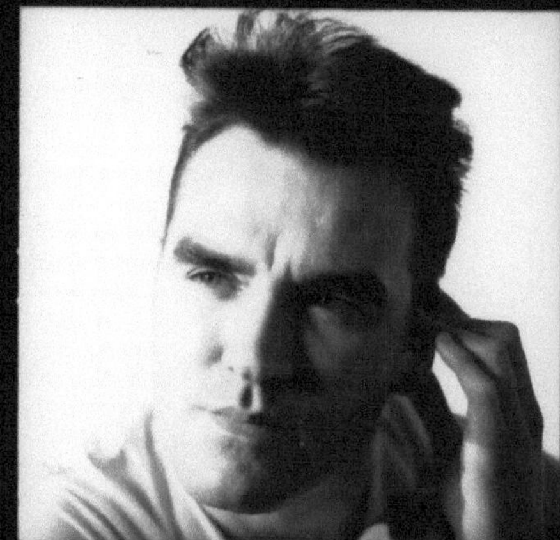

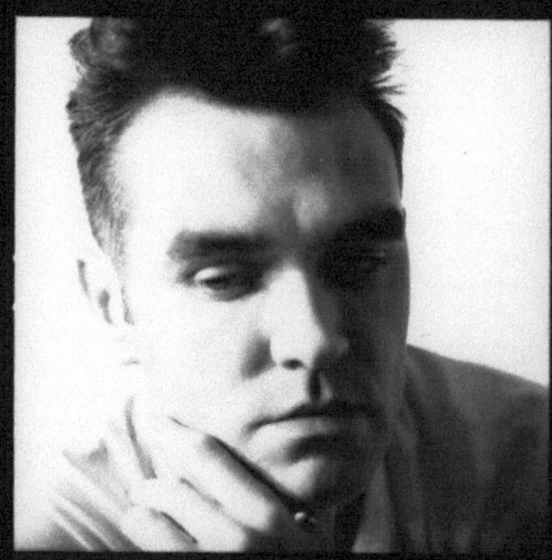

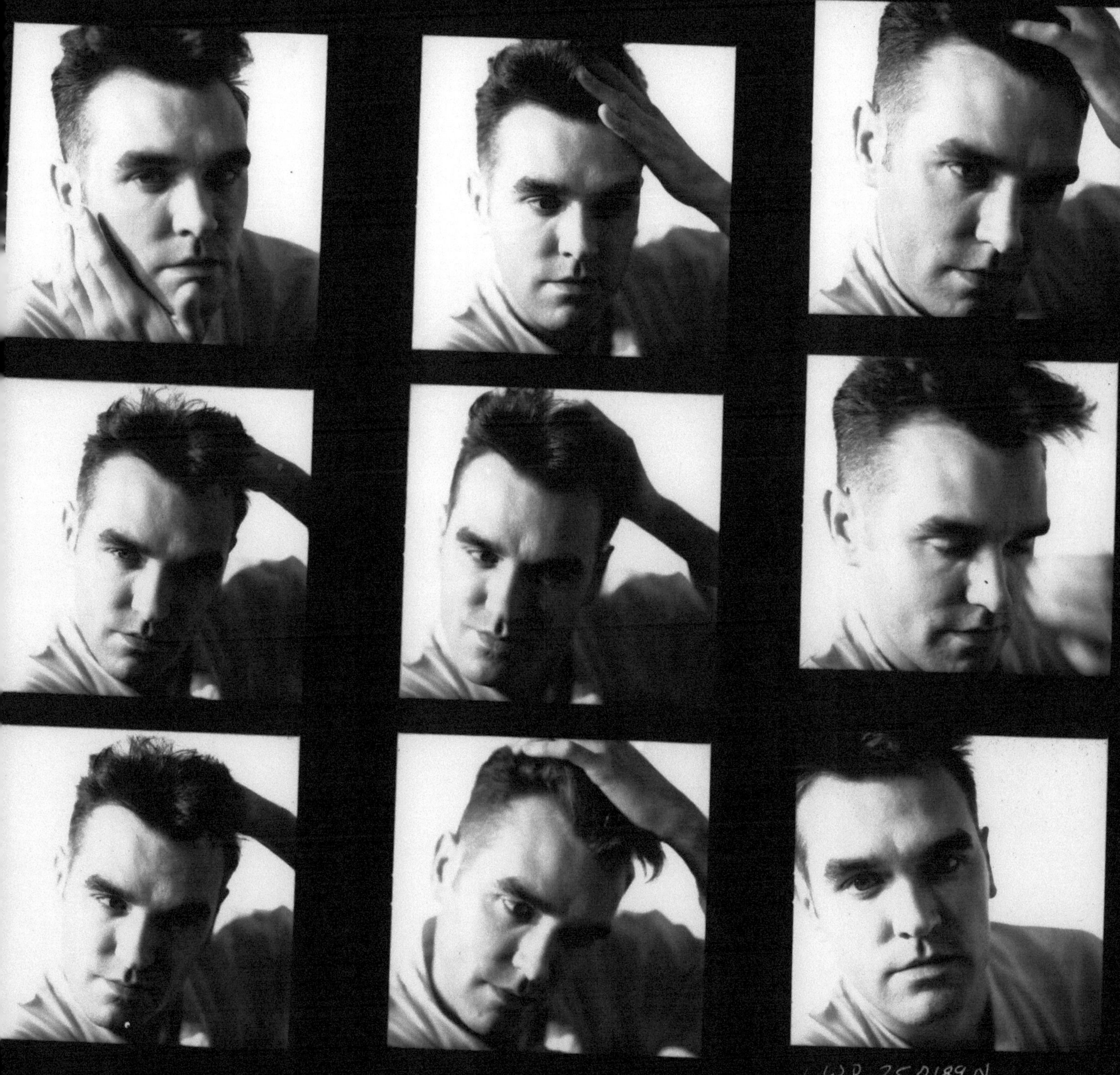
L.W.P. 25 0189 N

He looks like a Hollywood matinee idol here.

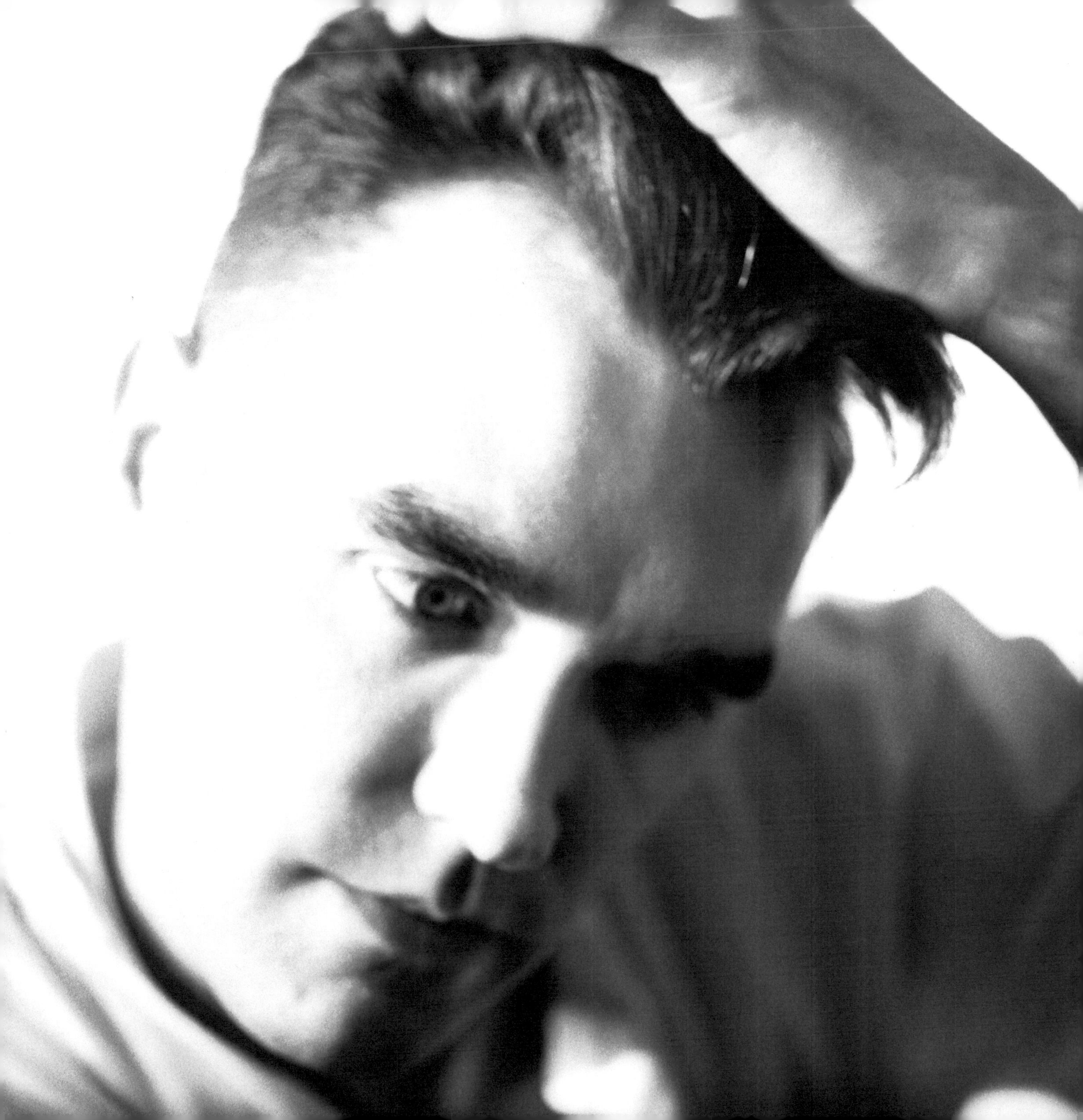

A friend at school had a dark room in Stamford Hill. He had a little camera and we all borrowed that and cheated on our art O levels. We took some pictures around scrap yards to print out and put them on an overhead projector which we copied for the exam. I enjoyed it from the start and the dark room was exciting. My step-mum and dad said that I wasn't going to doss around and do A levels, I had to get a job. Because I quite enjoyed the experience I'd had I found a YOP scheme in a dark room, doing a bit of everything – black-and-white printing, black-and-white and colour processing, colour neg, colour slides and printing. I learned about the whole thing. I wanted to be a photojournalist, a Magnum photographer and go out and change the world. I was a young punk rocker who would put the world to rights, so I took the camera out on the Anti-Nazi League marches and H-Block marches. The pictures weren't great but I was enthusiastic. Then I got a job in a dark room at London Weekend Television. I enjoyed the whole process of taking photographs, but always got as much enjoyment out of the processing and printing. It just seemed a nice, interesting way to make a living. About a year and a half into that, my step-brother Dave Dorrell was doing some journalism work, doing concert reviews and I started going along with him, taking live pictures and eventually I started submitting them. The first one was Southern Death Cult, and Paul Du Noyer, he was the live editor at the *NME*, picked one of the prints and ran it. But then the next one, Joe Jackson at the Hammersmith Odeon was my first commission and I turned up, but my name wasn't on the guest list and I couldn't get in and I panicked and thought, *What do I do?* I just took a photo of his name on the sign outside. I thought that was it, the end of my career and I went to Paul to explain and he shrugged and said, "Don't worry. It happens." I think my next one was Nico at the Venue in Victoria and that was it.

But I was still learning, still a bit naïve, still a bit intimidated. I only had one lens then and it was a wide one, so when it was in the pit I needed to get up close and that was useful. The first time I remember really being pleased with what I'd done was the first feature I did for the *NME* – Smiley Culture and Asher Senator at the time of "Cockney Translation". It should have been Papa Levi in the picture as well but he was three hours late, so that was an early lesson in the time-keeping of reggae artists.

I'd know in the dark room more than when was taking it that I'd got that image right. I started getting enough work from commissions that I could make a living from it, and it was a decision – do I want to work in the dark room or as a photographer? But it was simply that I was enjoying it, getting lovely trips abroad, I loved music and the musicians that I was working with. In fact when I was a teenager I'd wanted to be a musician, and took lessons from the bass player in the UK Subs, but I was terrible, it took me six weeks to learn "Walk on the Wild Side" and even he said: "Are you sure this is for you?" So that was that. Actually they had a dark room in that youth club and I think even then I thought, *Photography, that could be the way to go: if I can't be in the band, I'll take pictures of the band.*

80

That looks like joyful play, but the writing was on the wall …

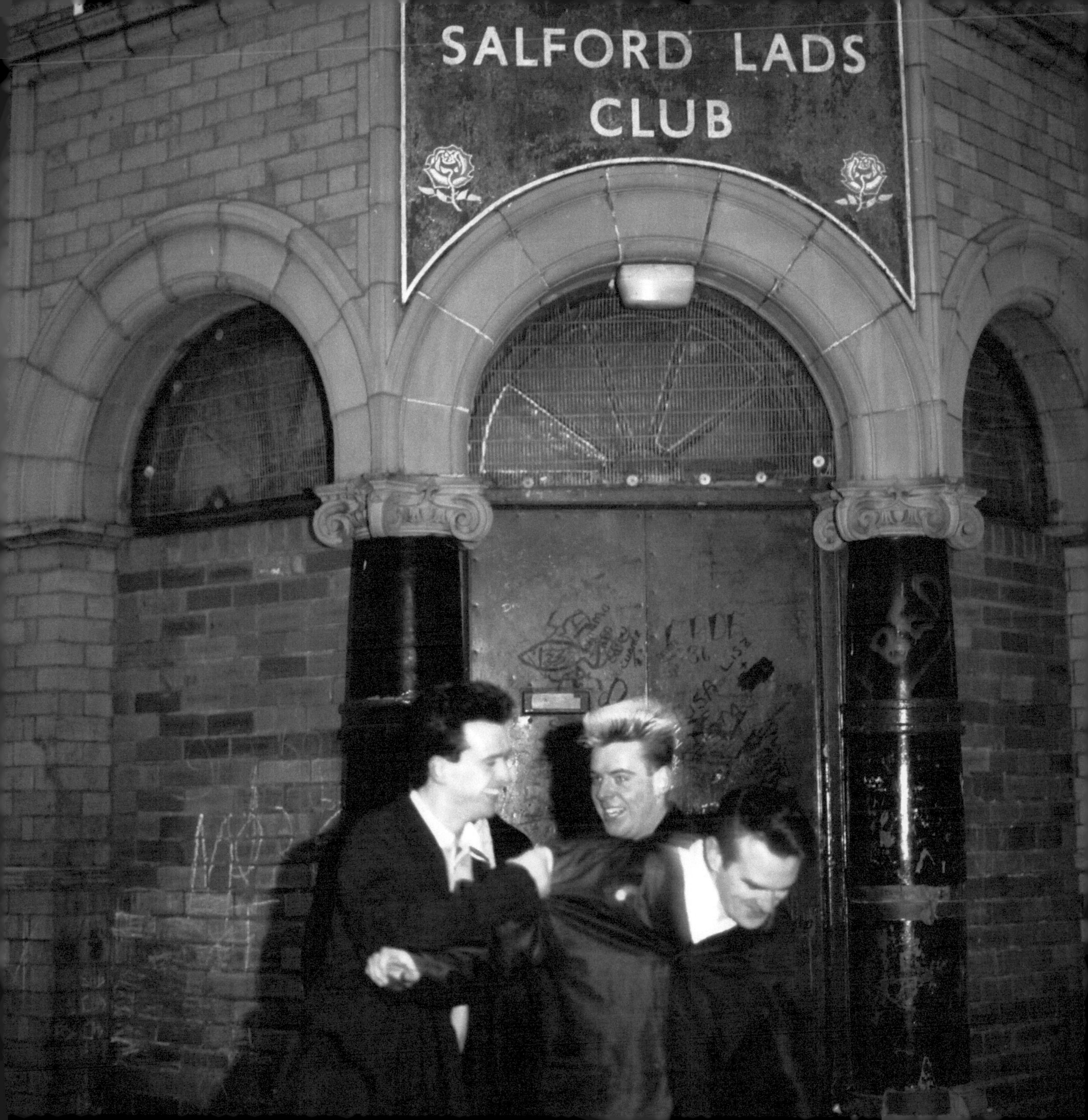
SALFORD LADS
CLUB

In front of the venue that will always be associated with The Smiths.

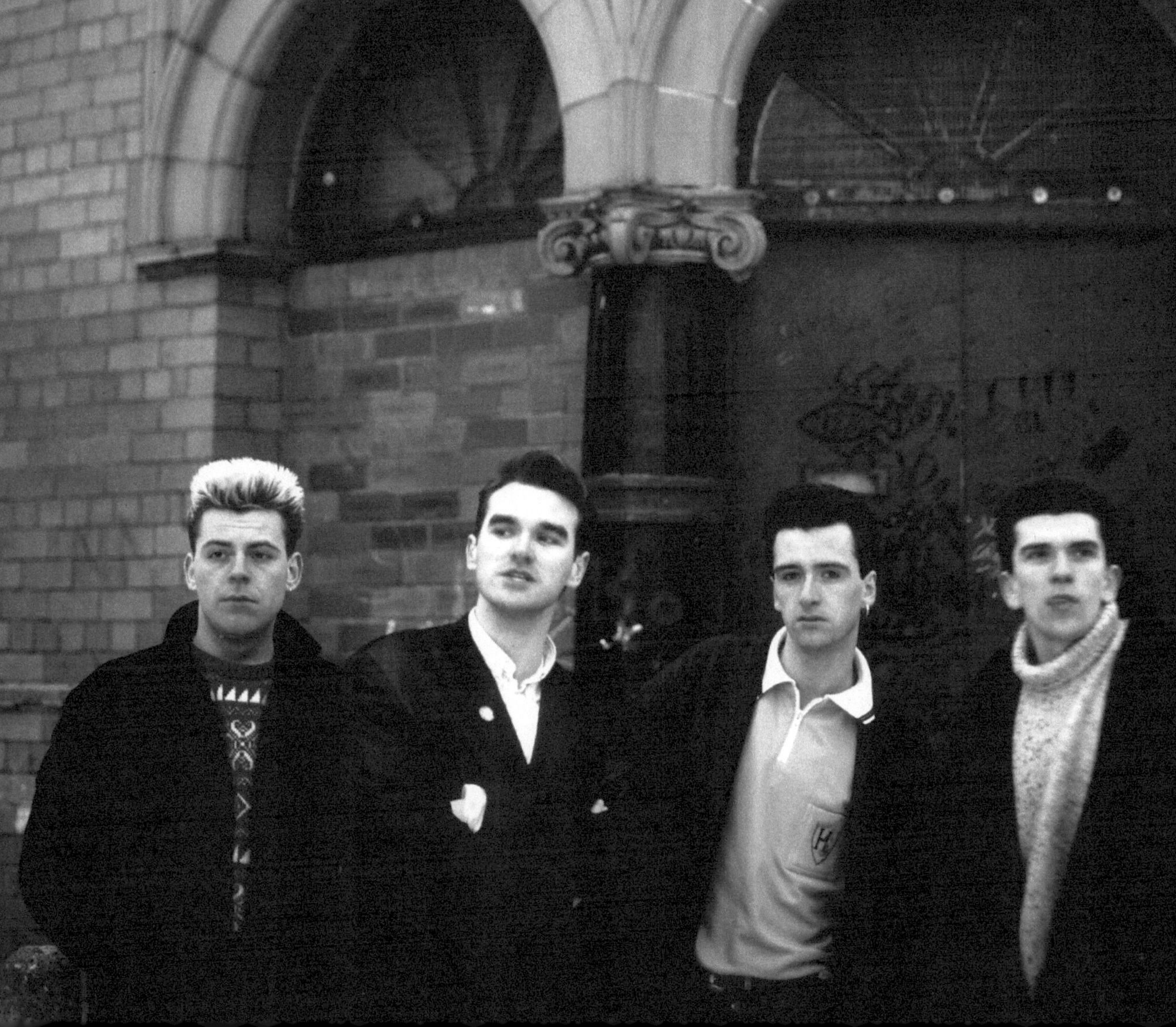
SALFORD LADS
CLUB

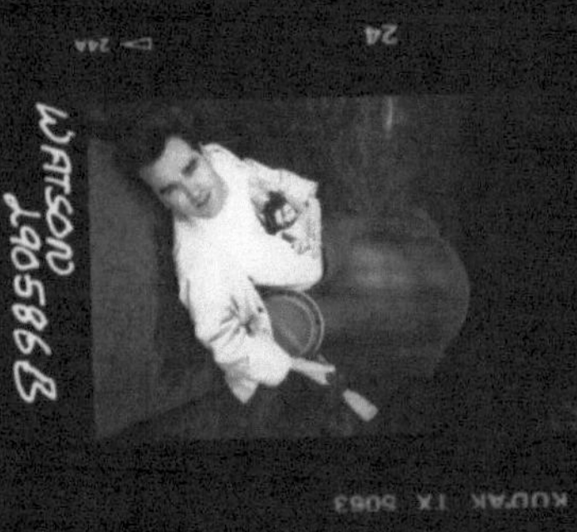

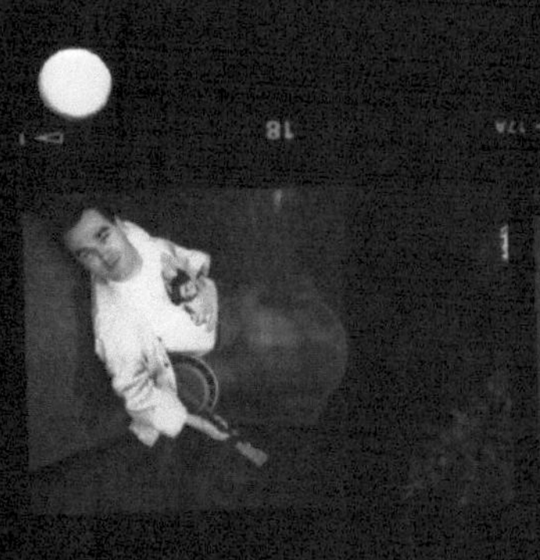

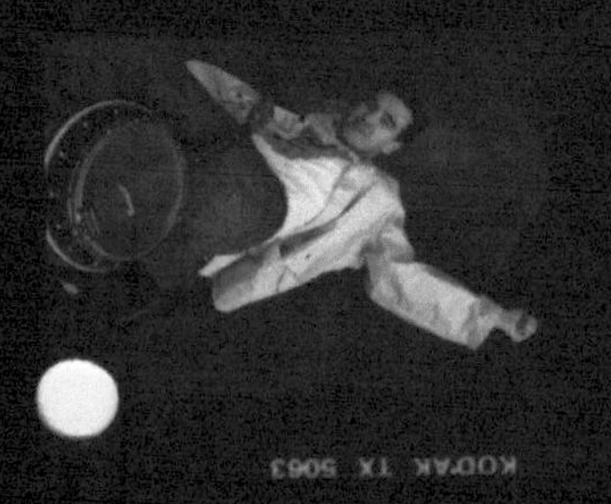

Morrissey at the Brompton Road cemetery. He'd brought along a banjolele in reference to one of his northern heroes, George Formby.

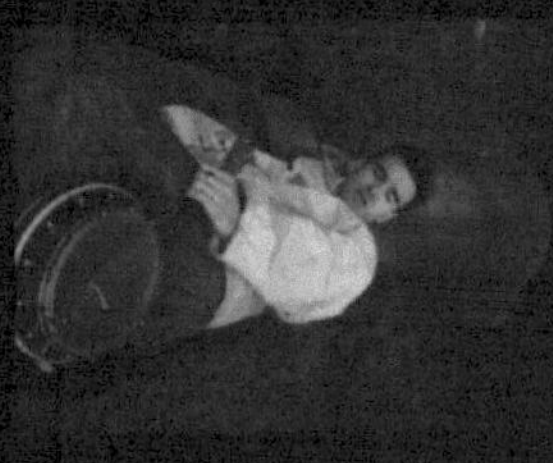

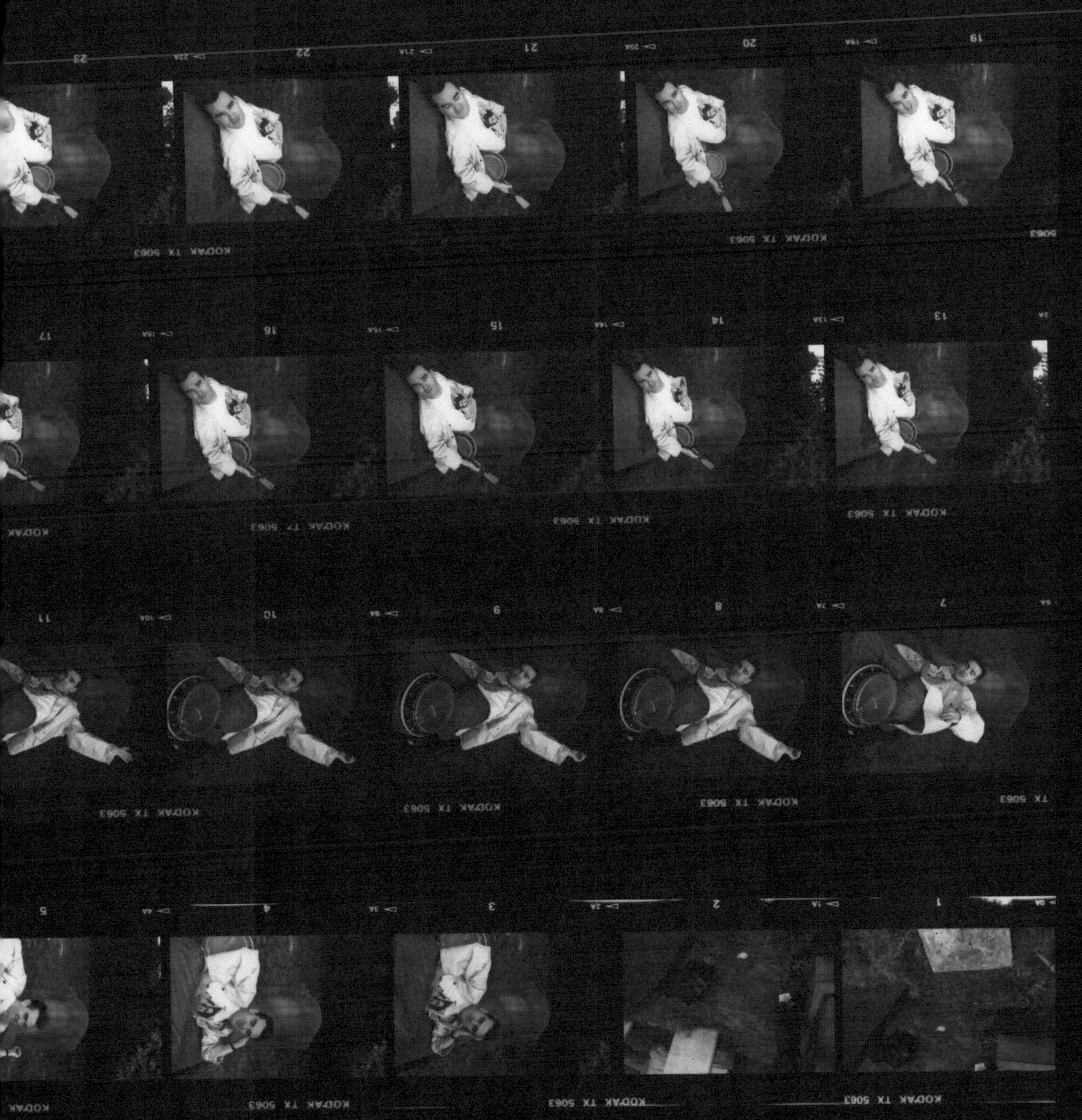

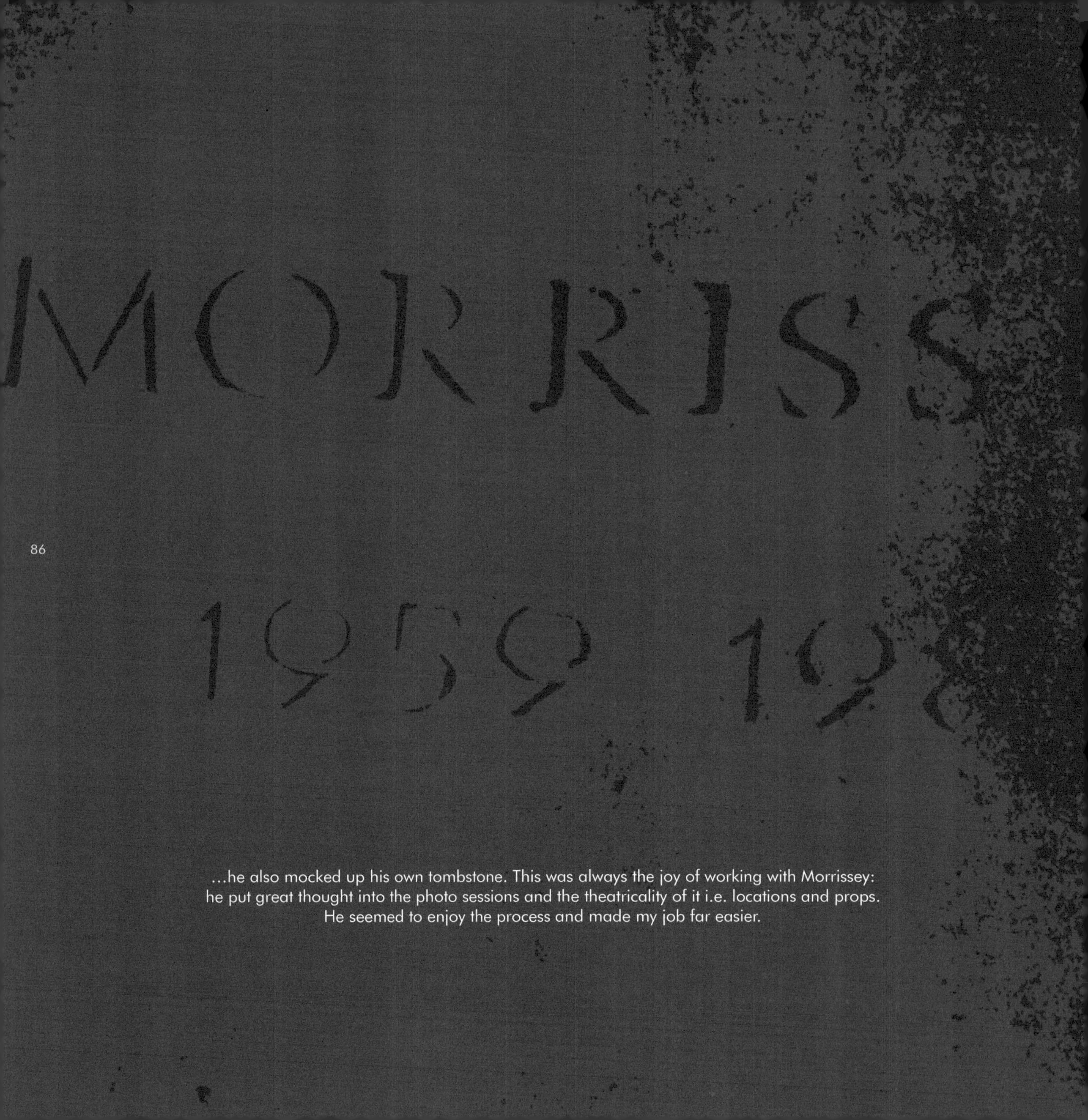

…he also mocked up his own tombstone. This was always the joy of working with Morrissey: he put great thought into the photo sessions and the theatricality of it i.e. locations and props. He seemed to enjoy the process and made my job far easier.

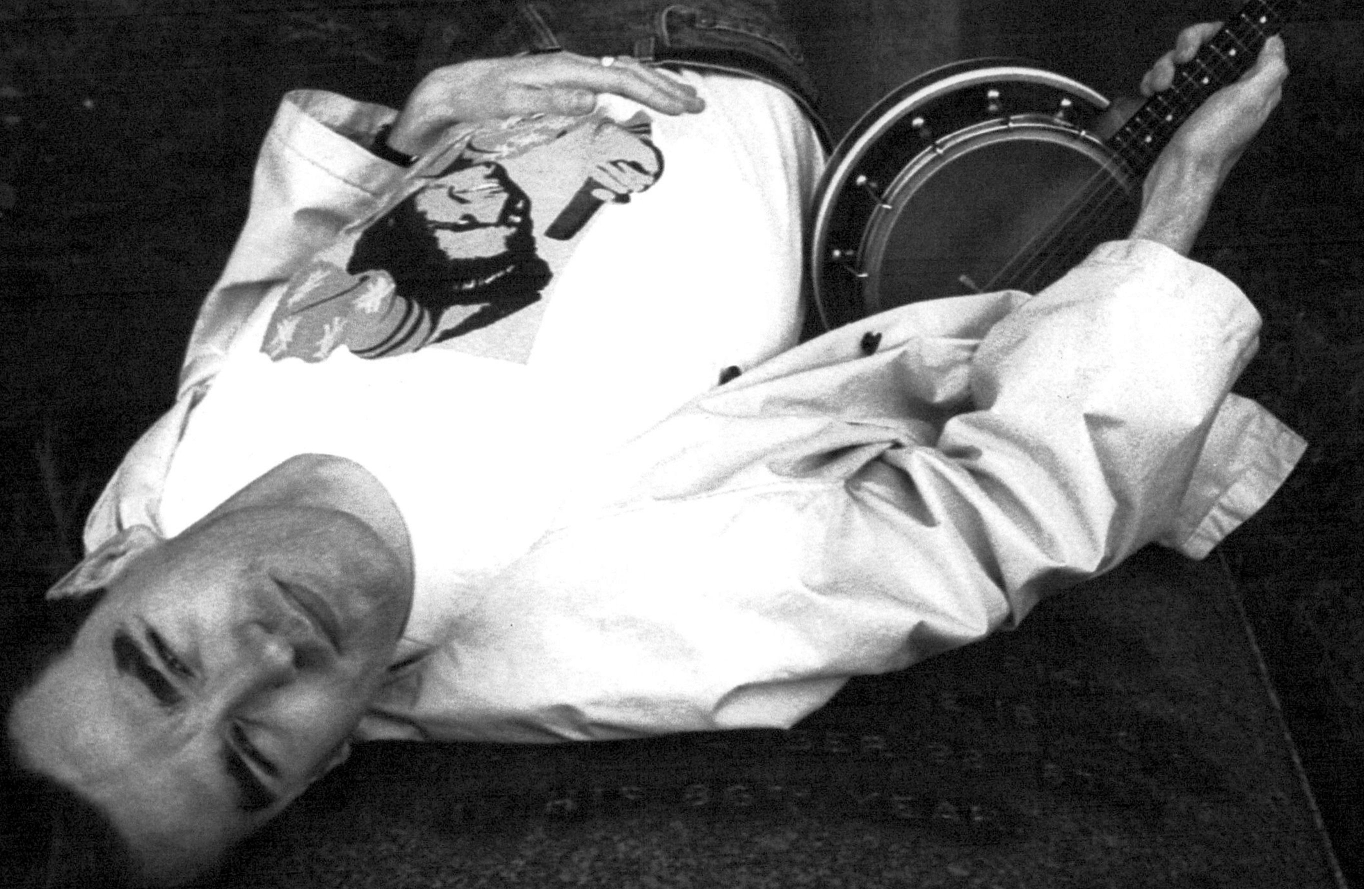
MORRISS
1959

MORRISSEY
1959 1986

ORRISS

1959 19

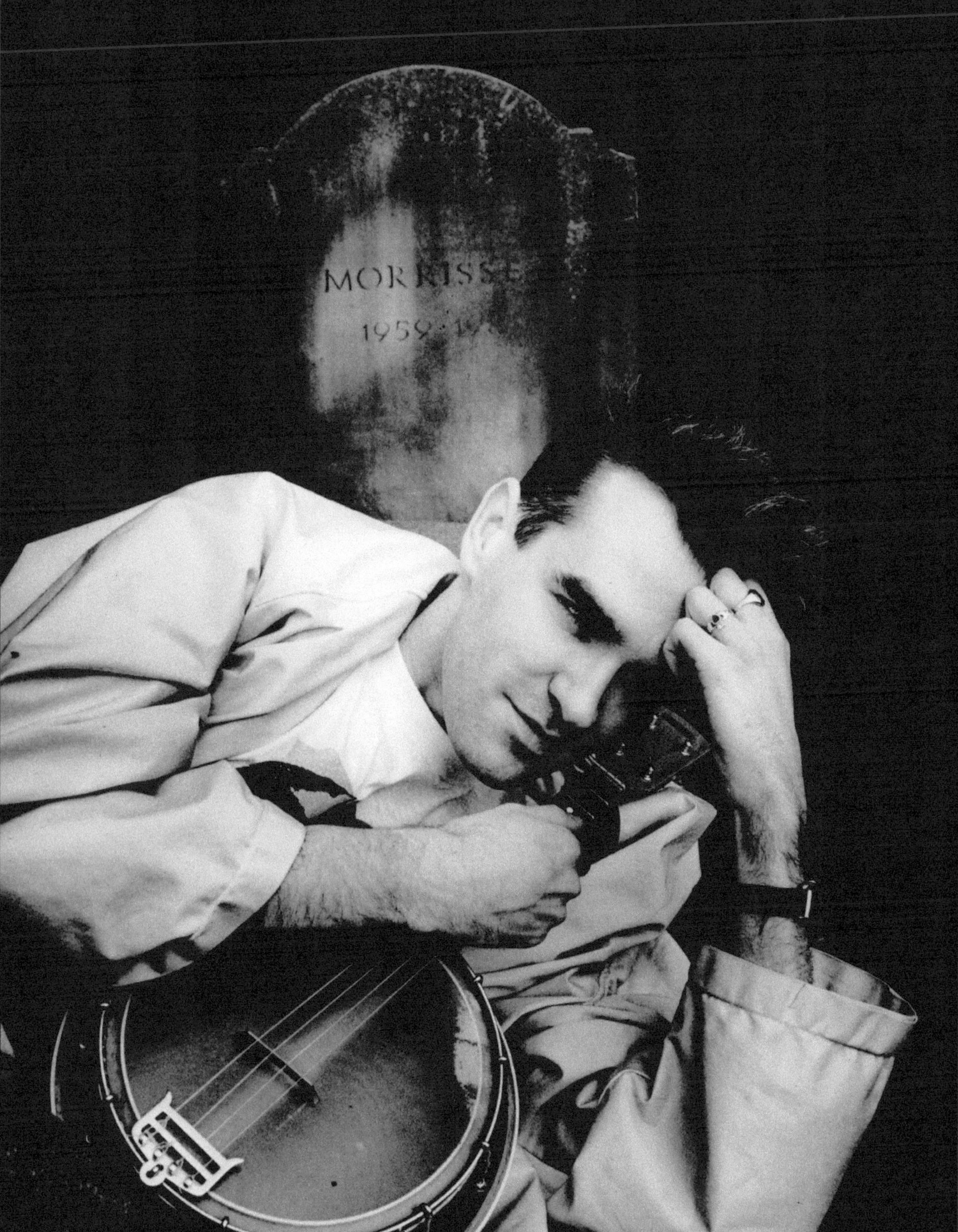
MORRISSE
1959

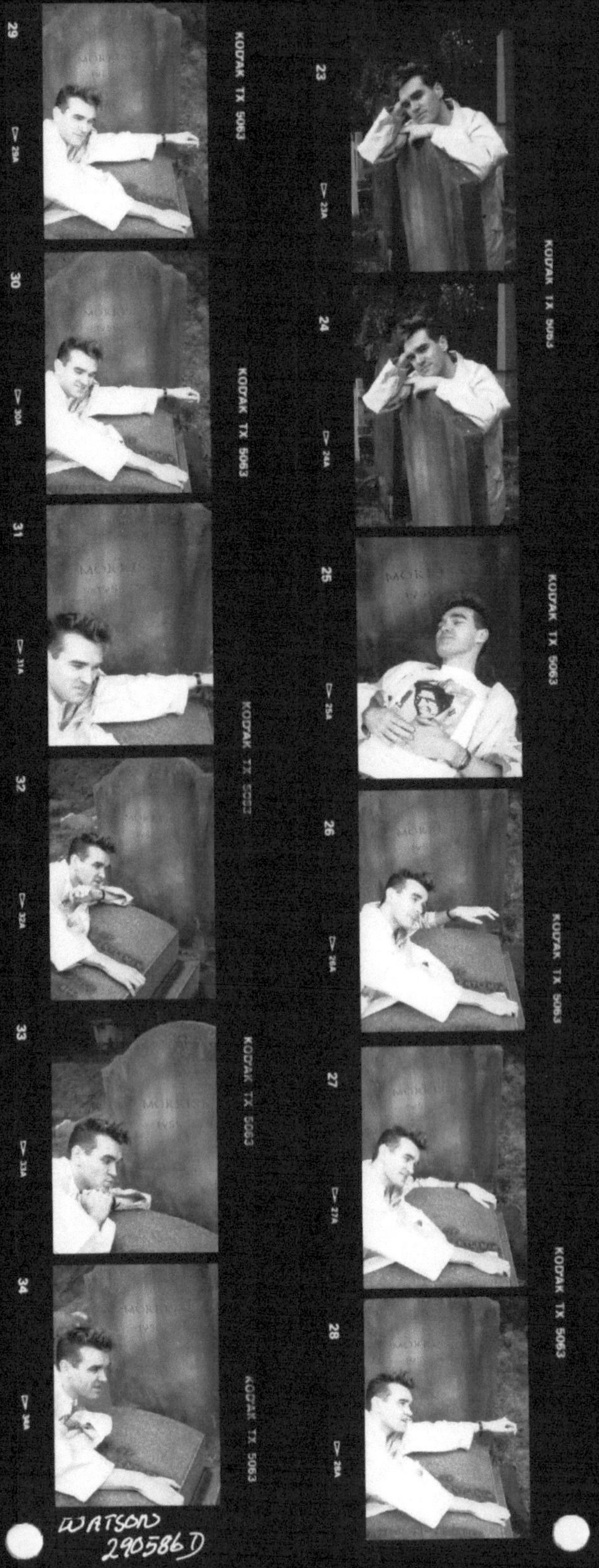
KODAK TX 5063
WATSON
290586D

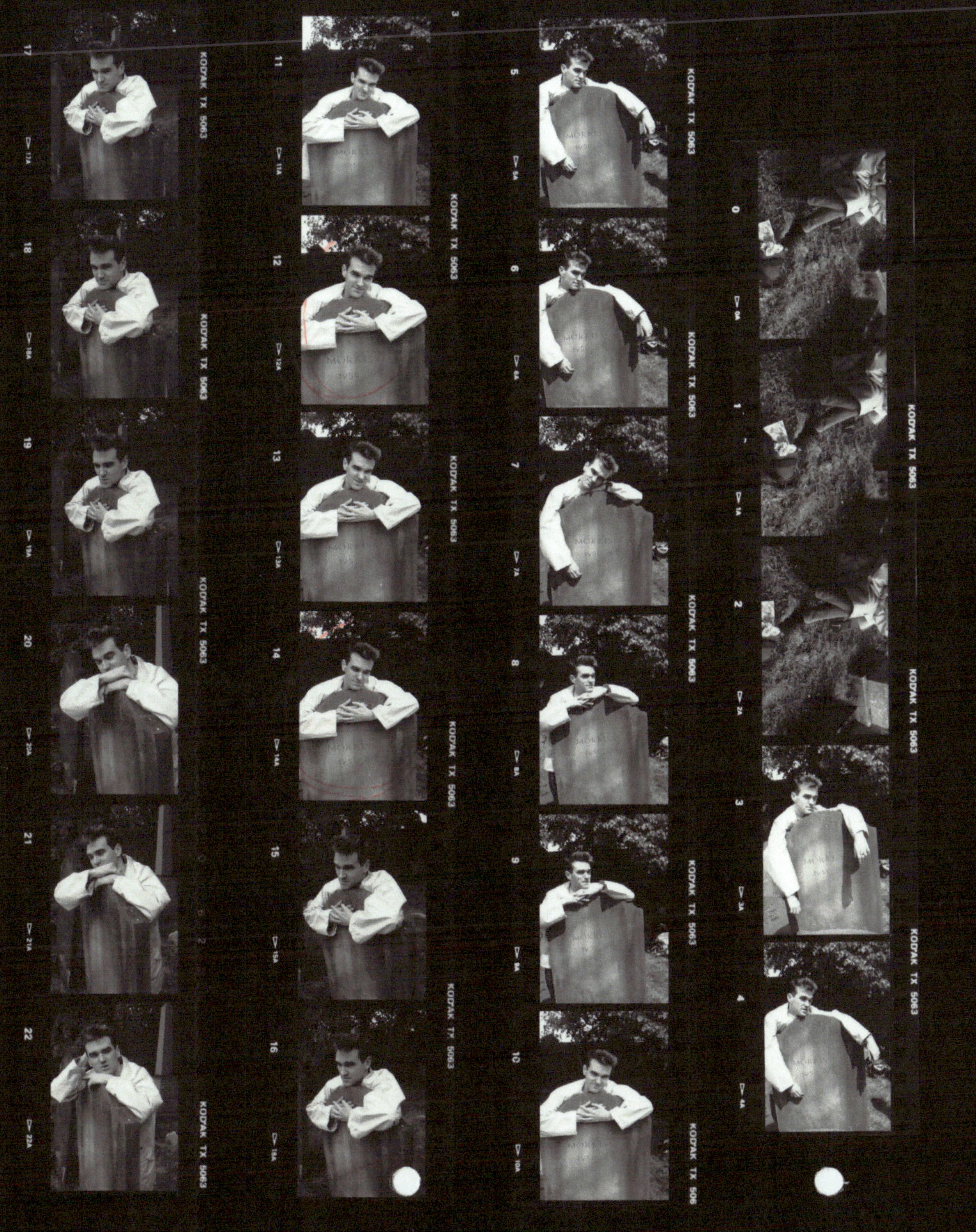
KODAK TX 5063

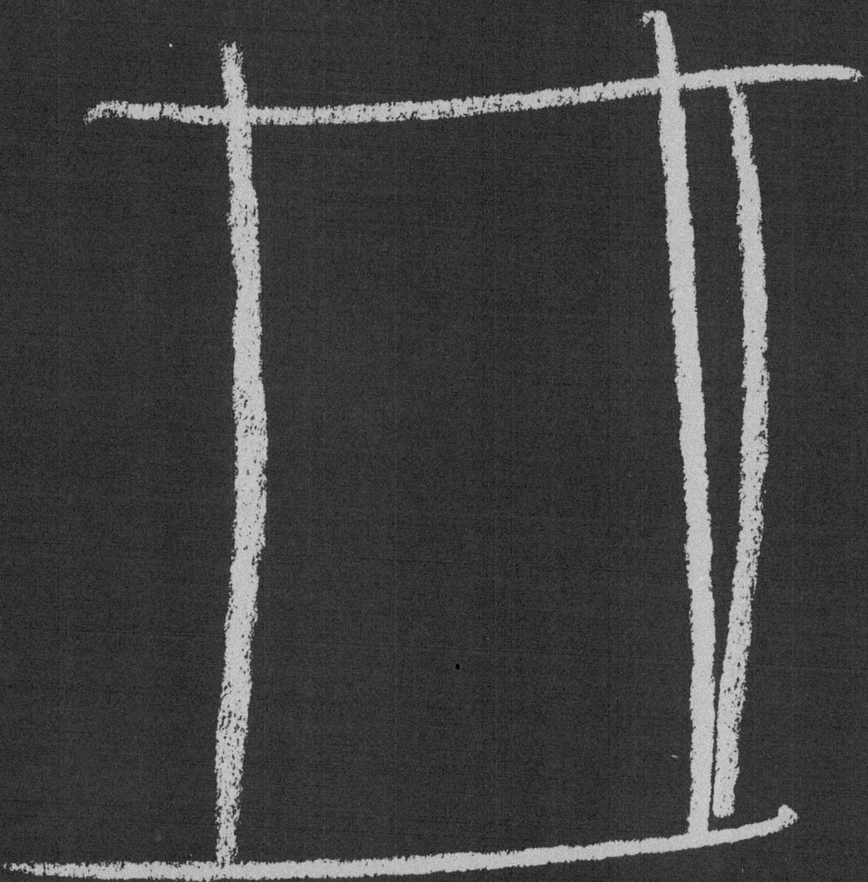

The Queen Is Not Dead.

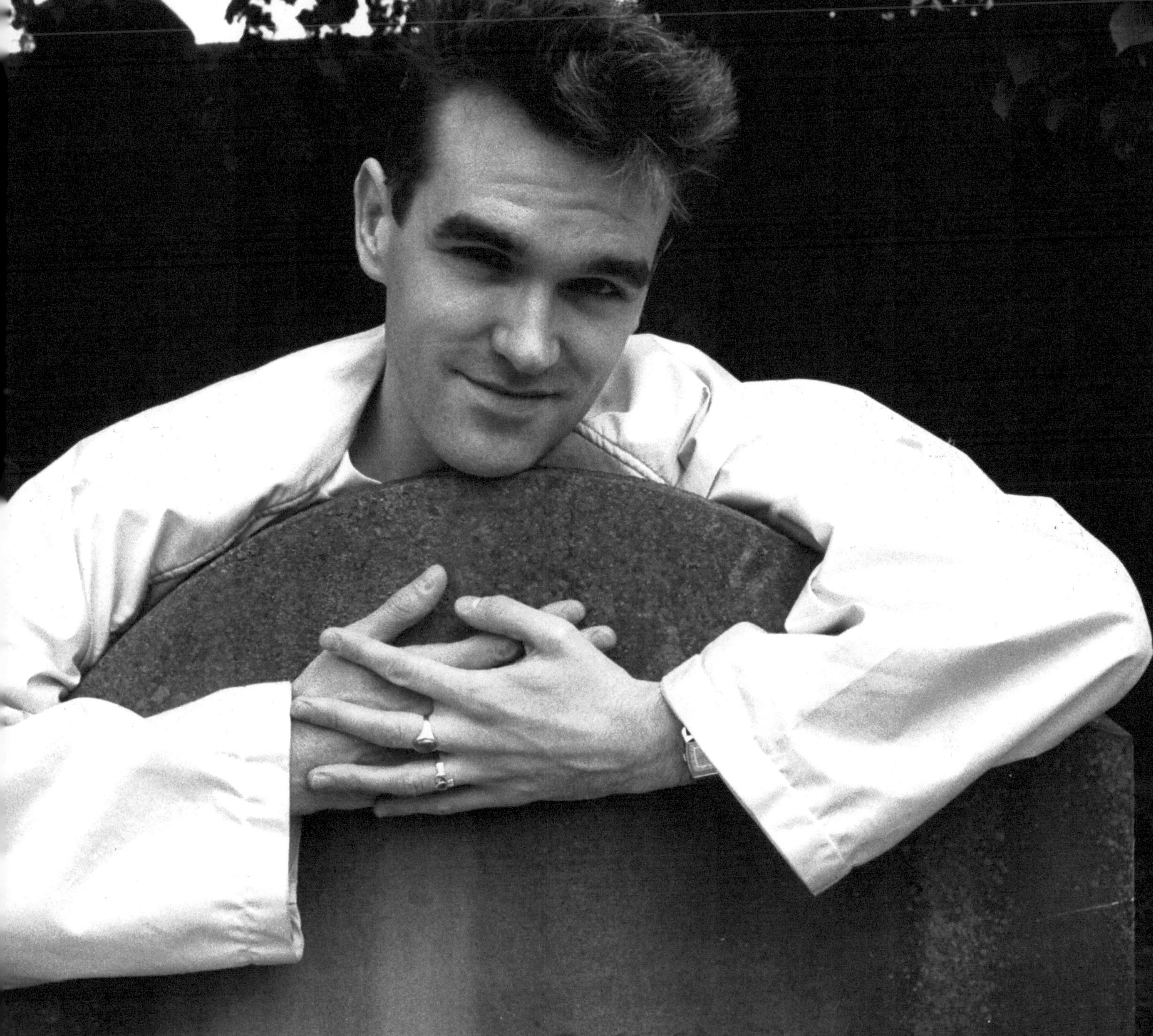
MORRISSE

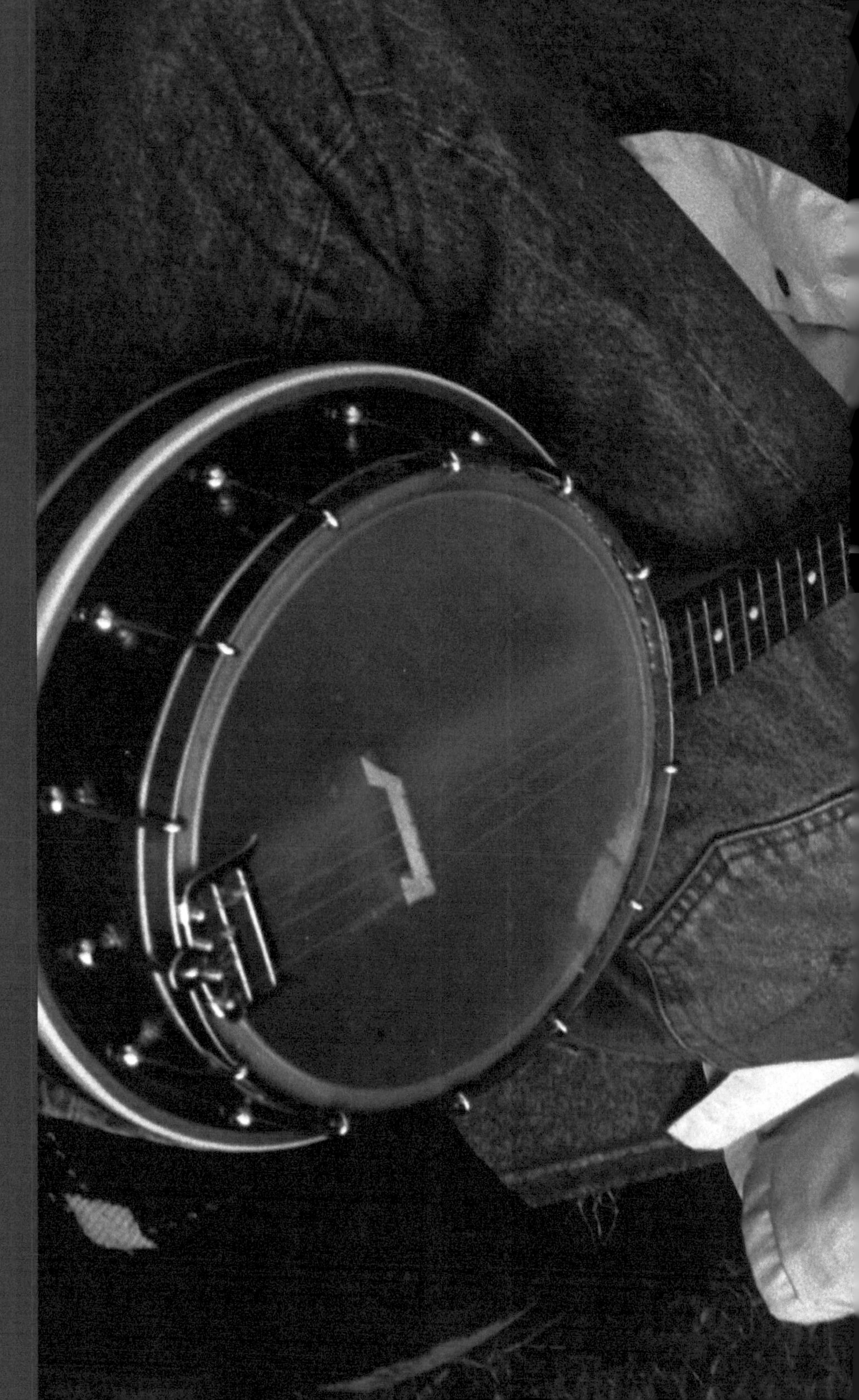

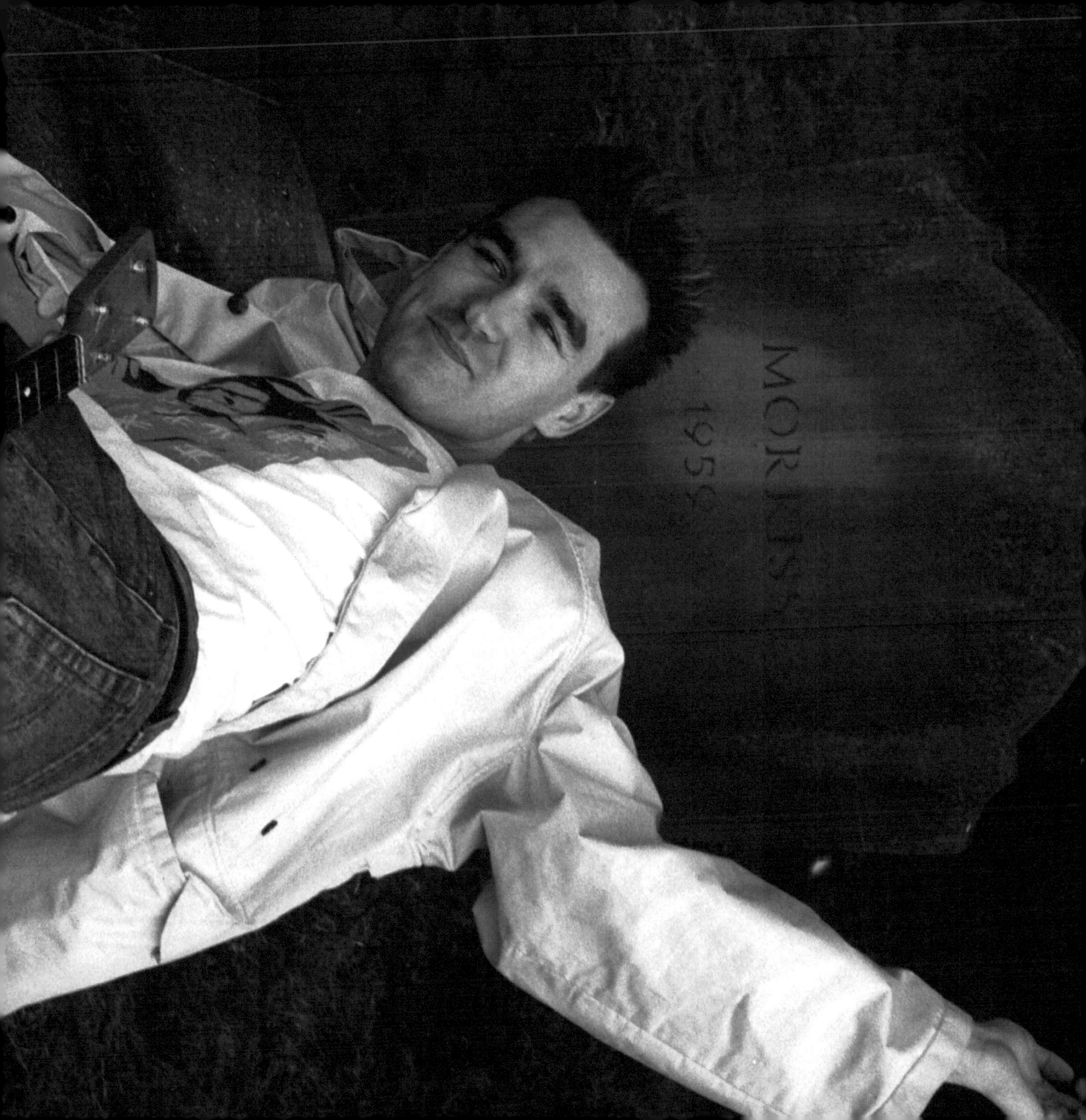

Cover session for *City Limits*, in Morrissey's flat in Chelsea.

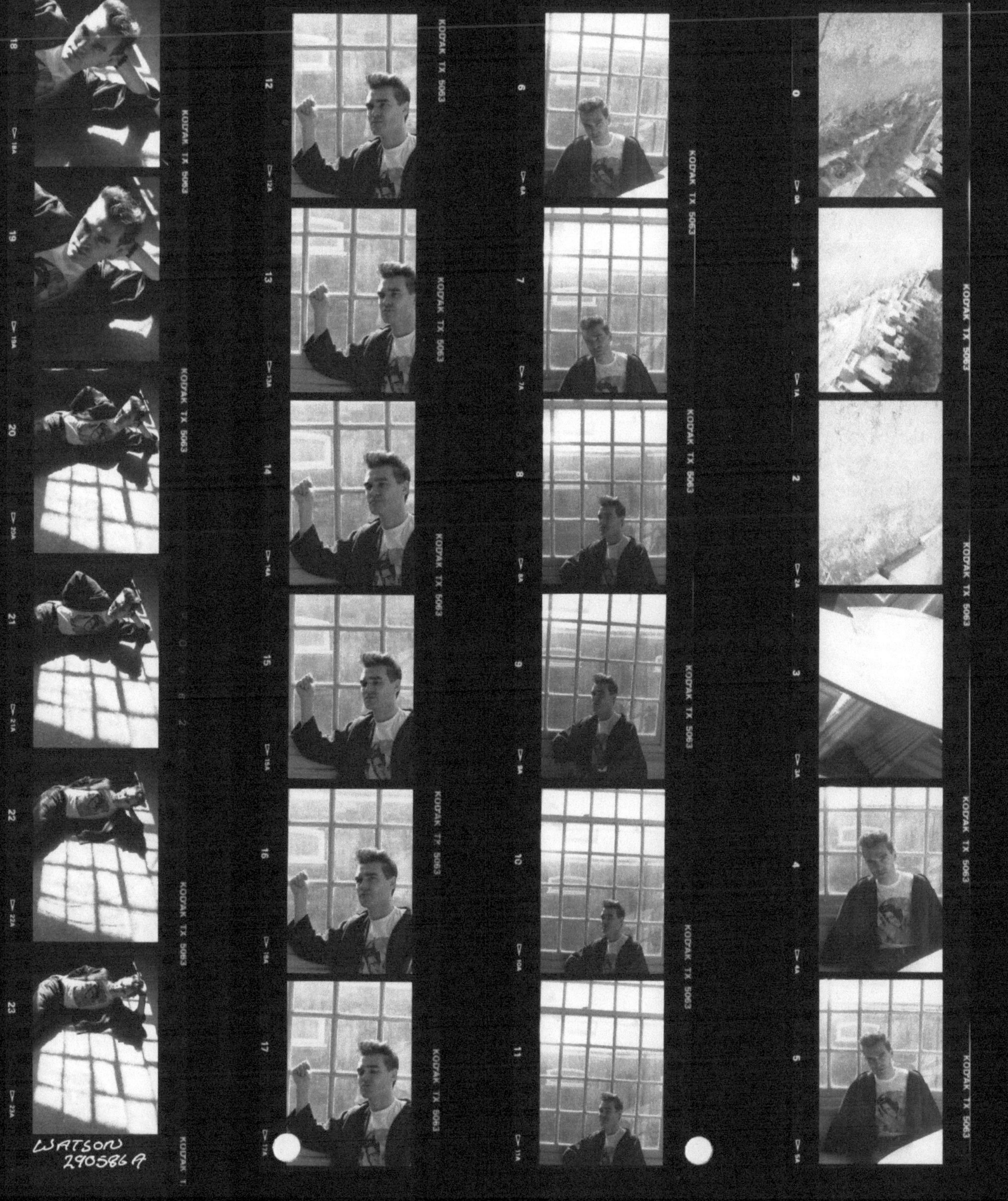

100

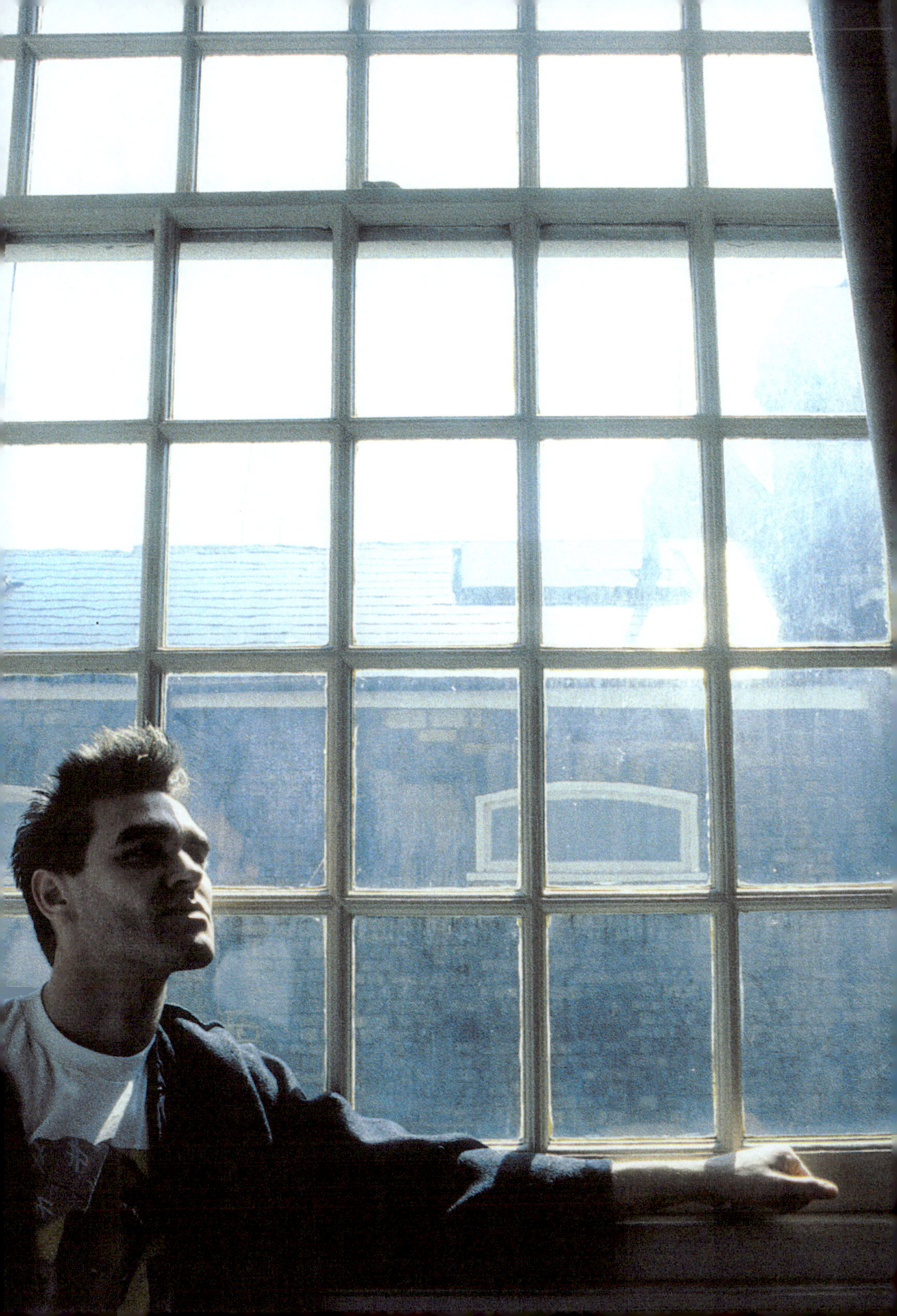

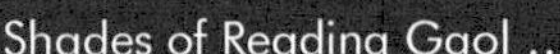

Shades of Reading Gaol …

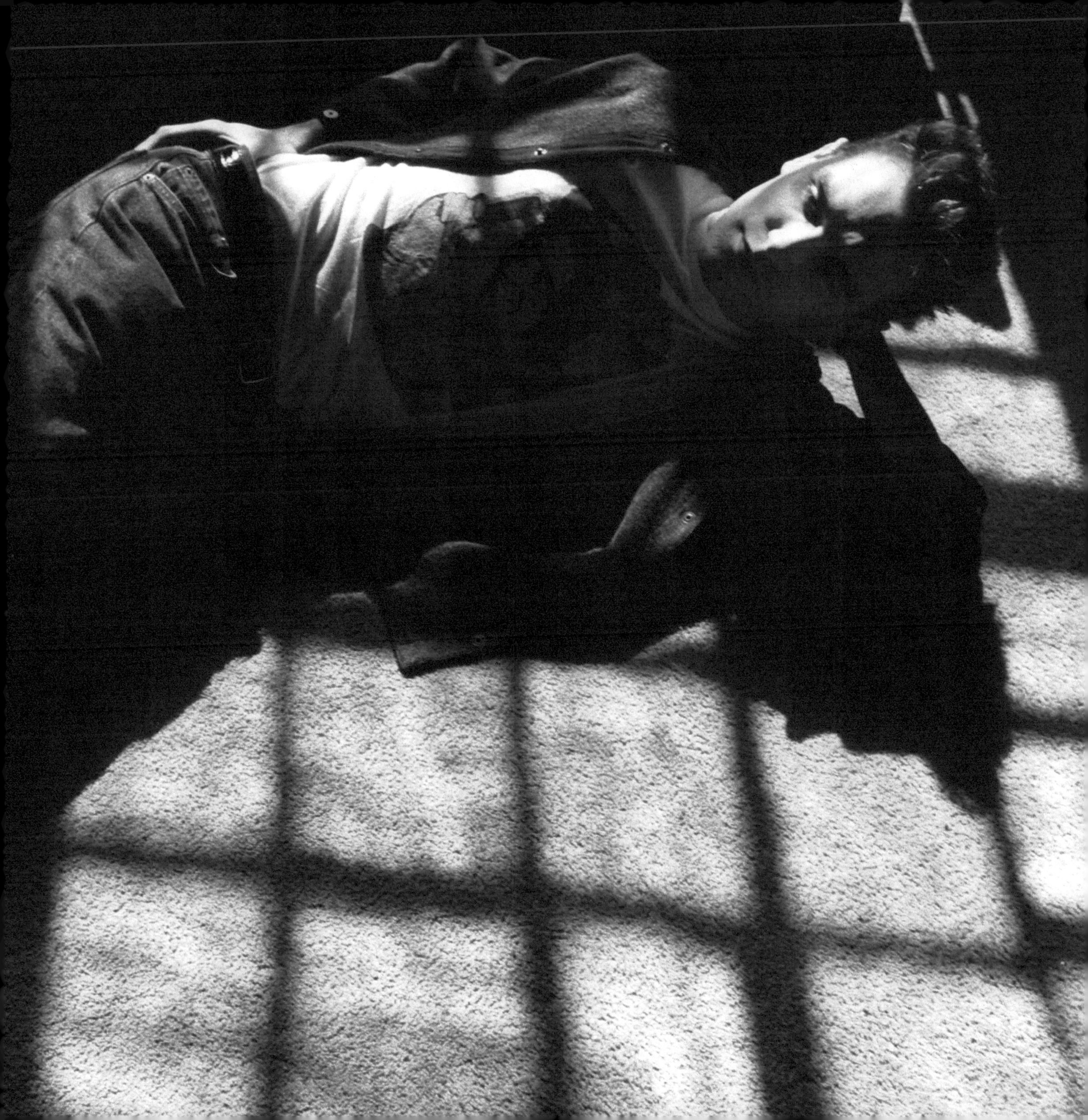

Morrissey sporting another of his idols.

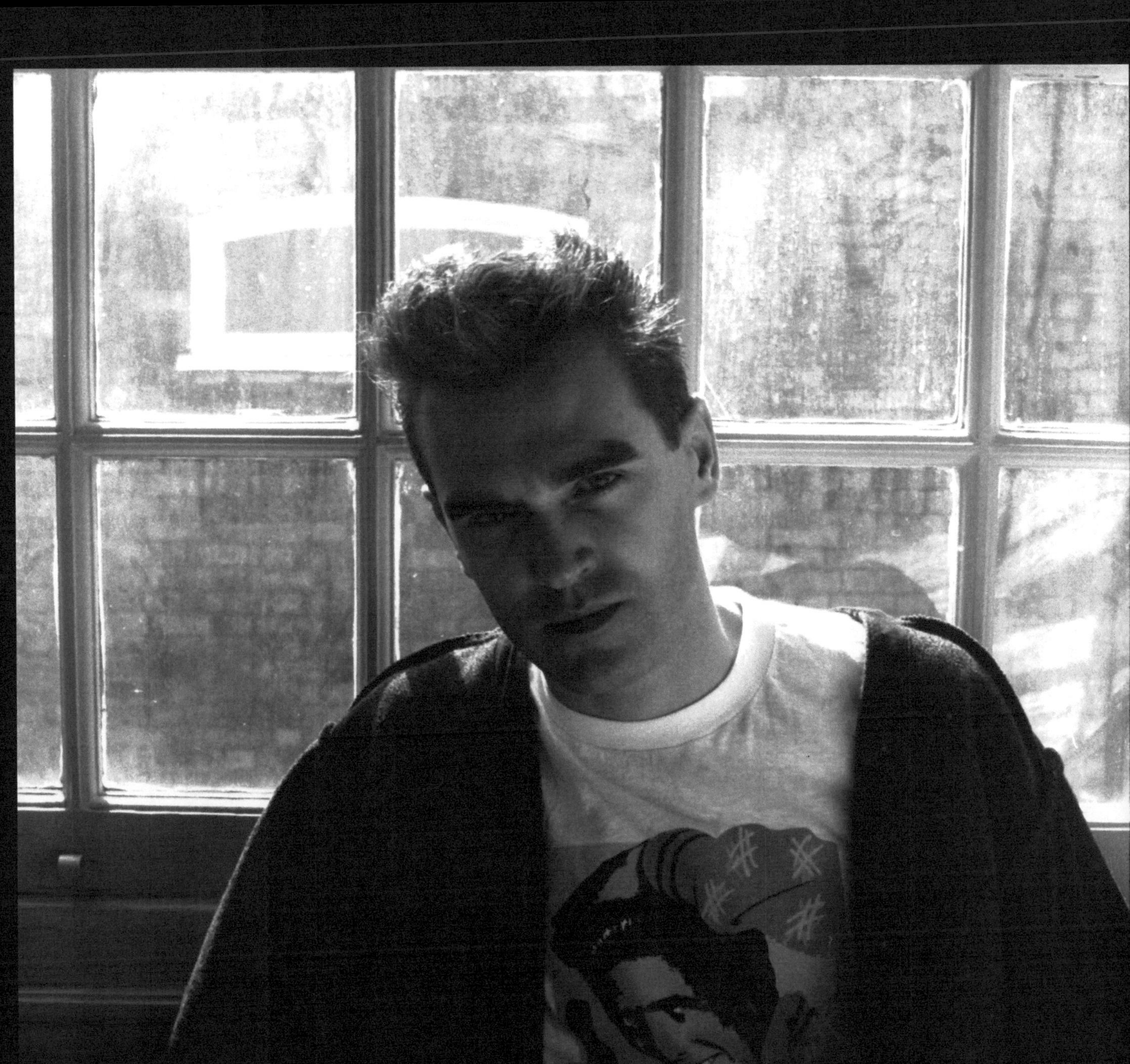

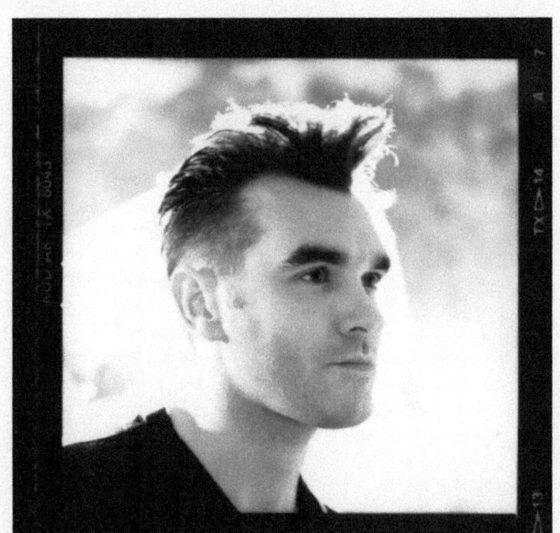

Black and white shots for the cover of "Interesting Drug".

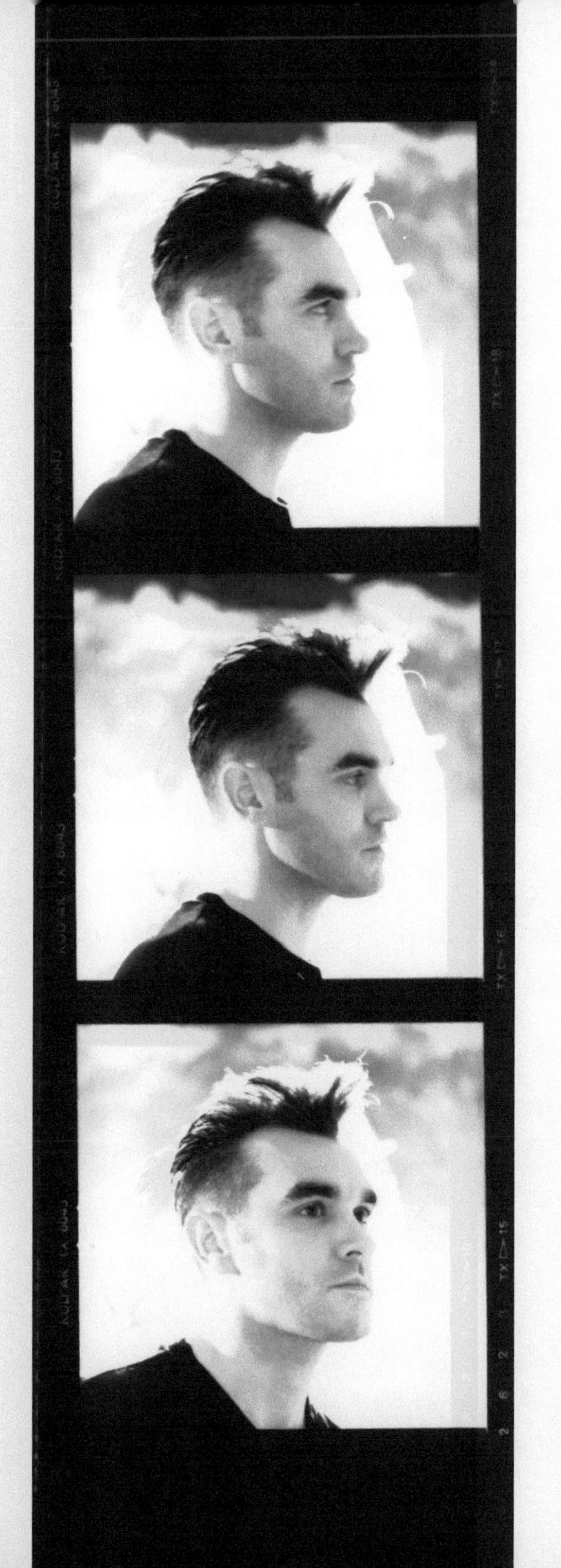

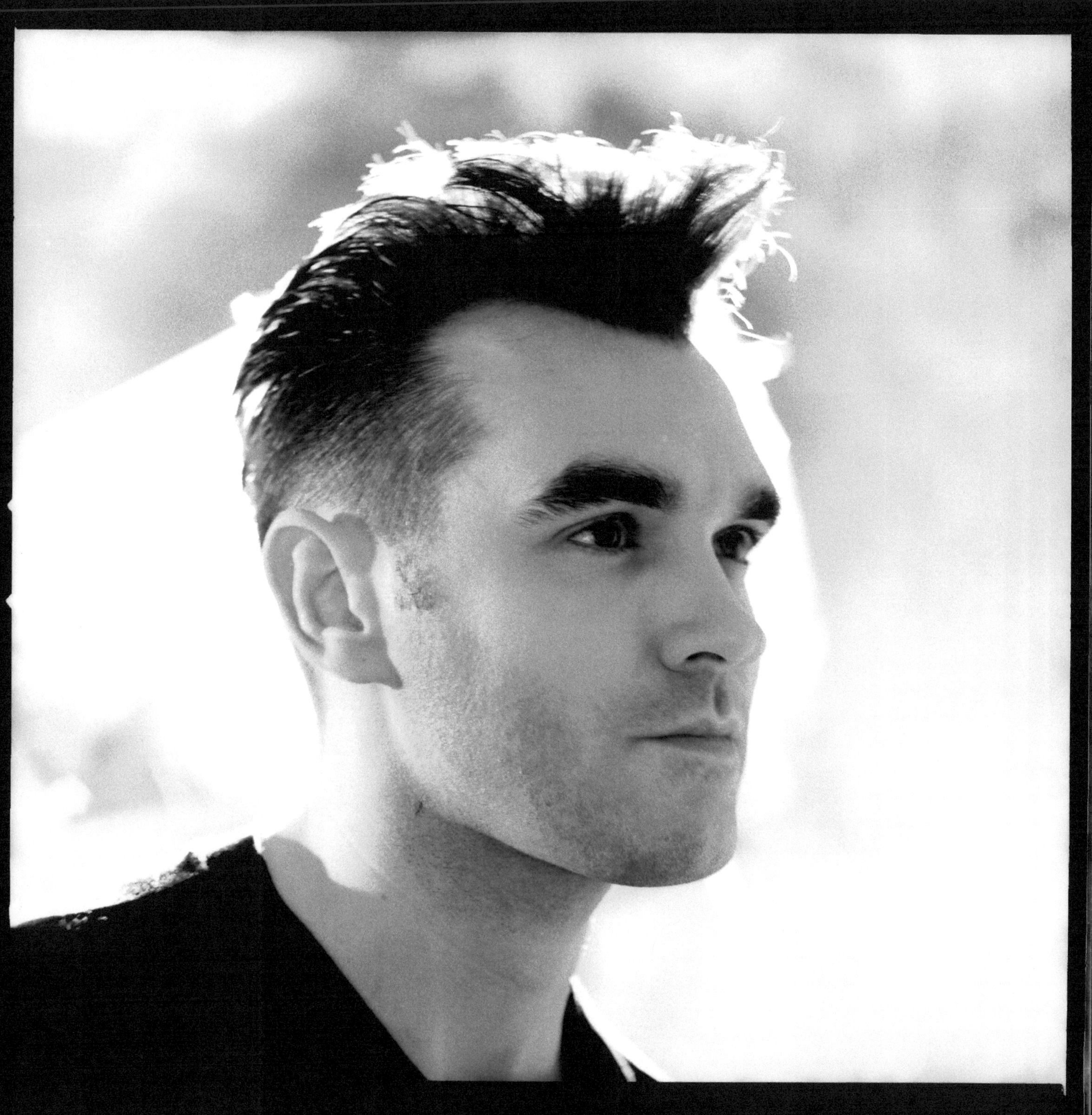

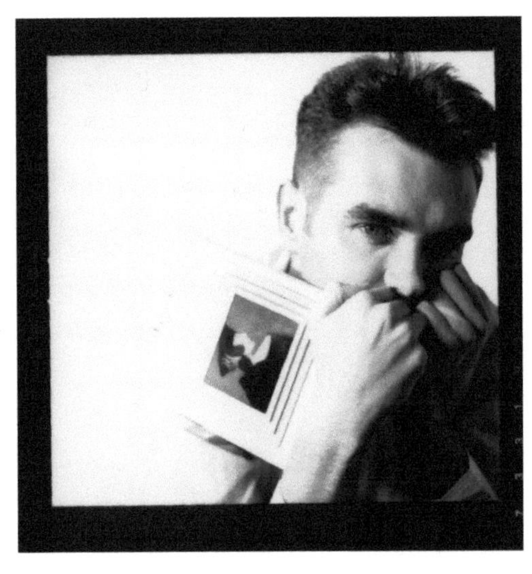

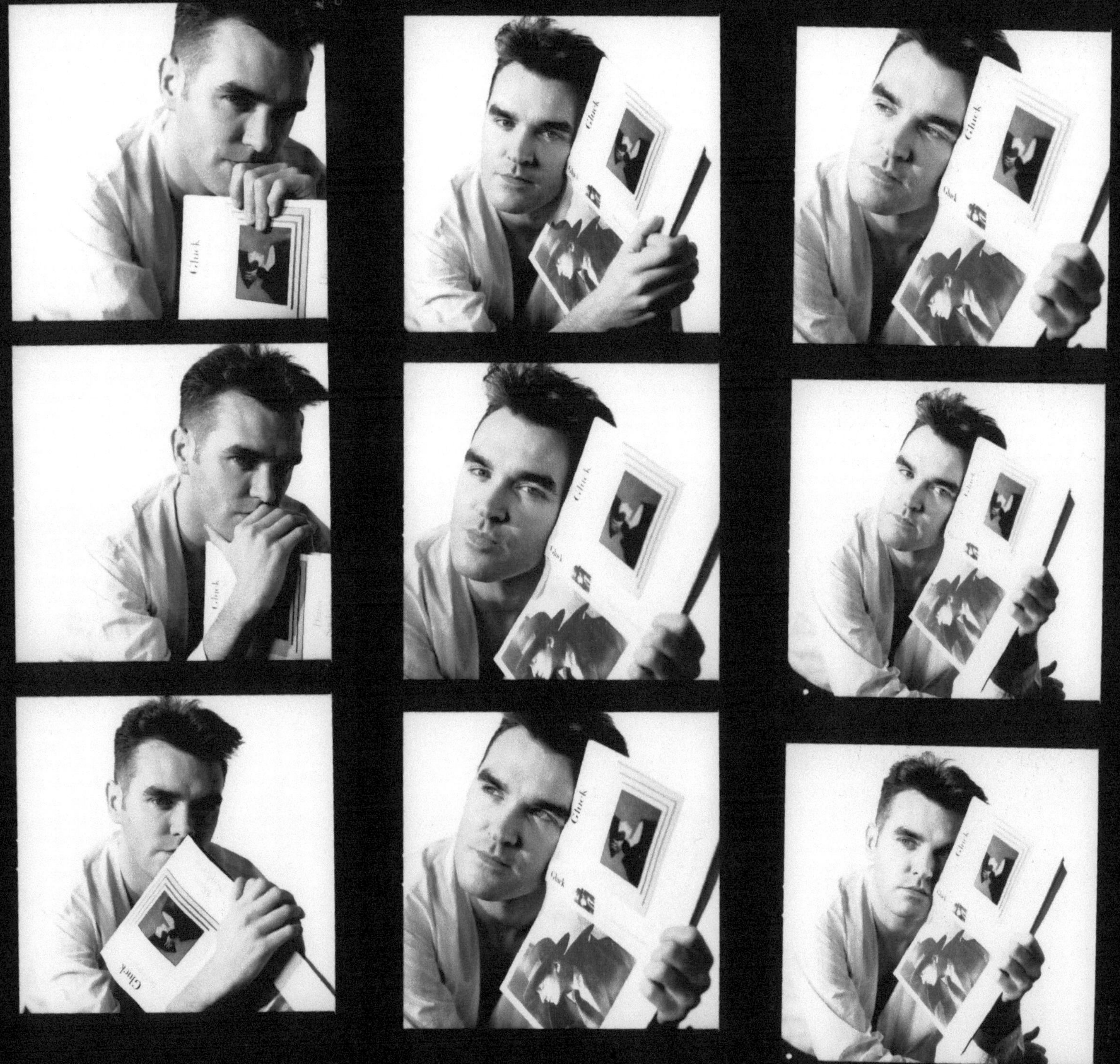
Gluck
Gluck
Gluck
Gluck
Gluck
Gluck
Gluck
Gluck
Gluck

Morrissey and Gluck.

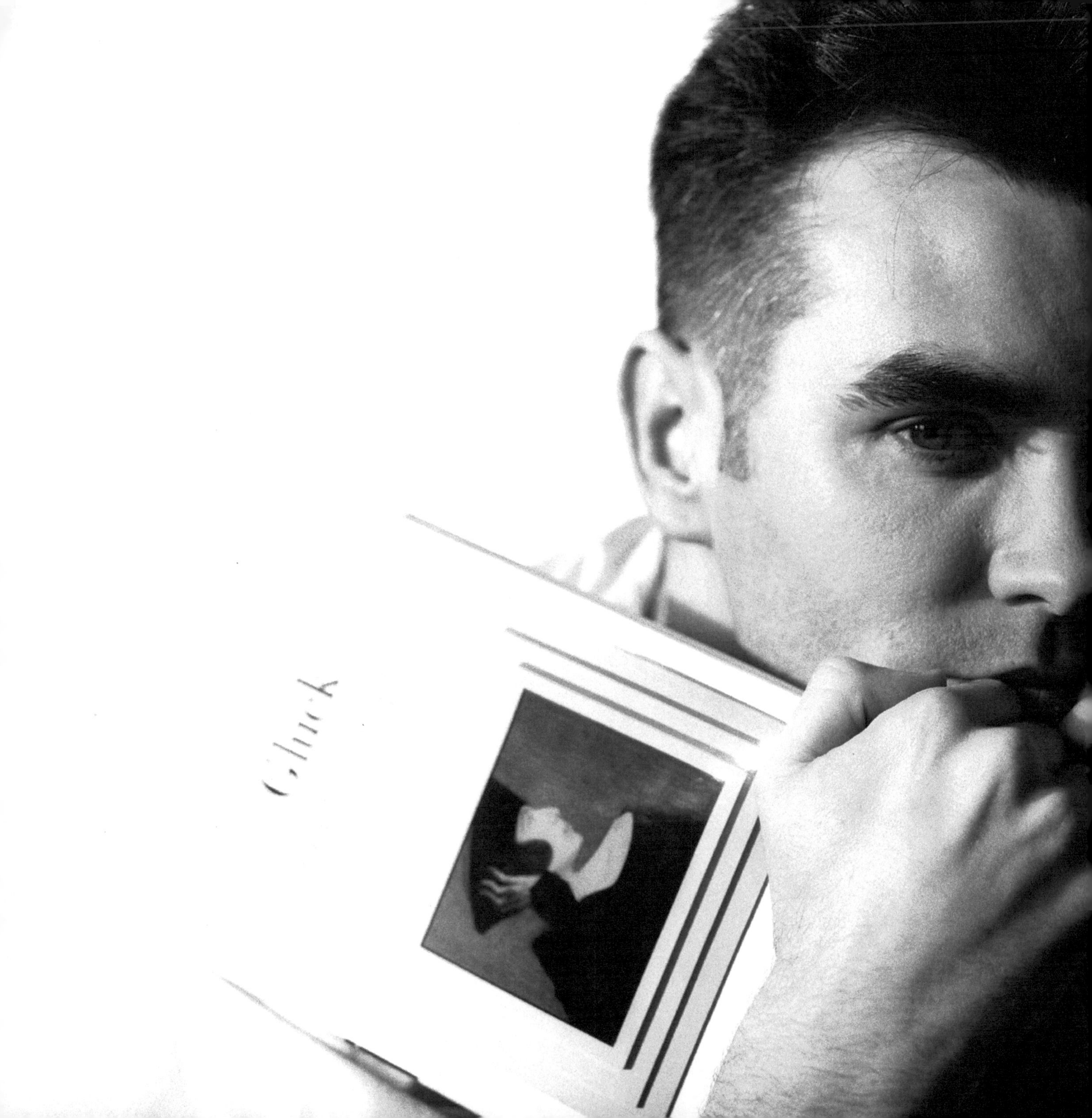
Gluck

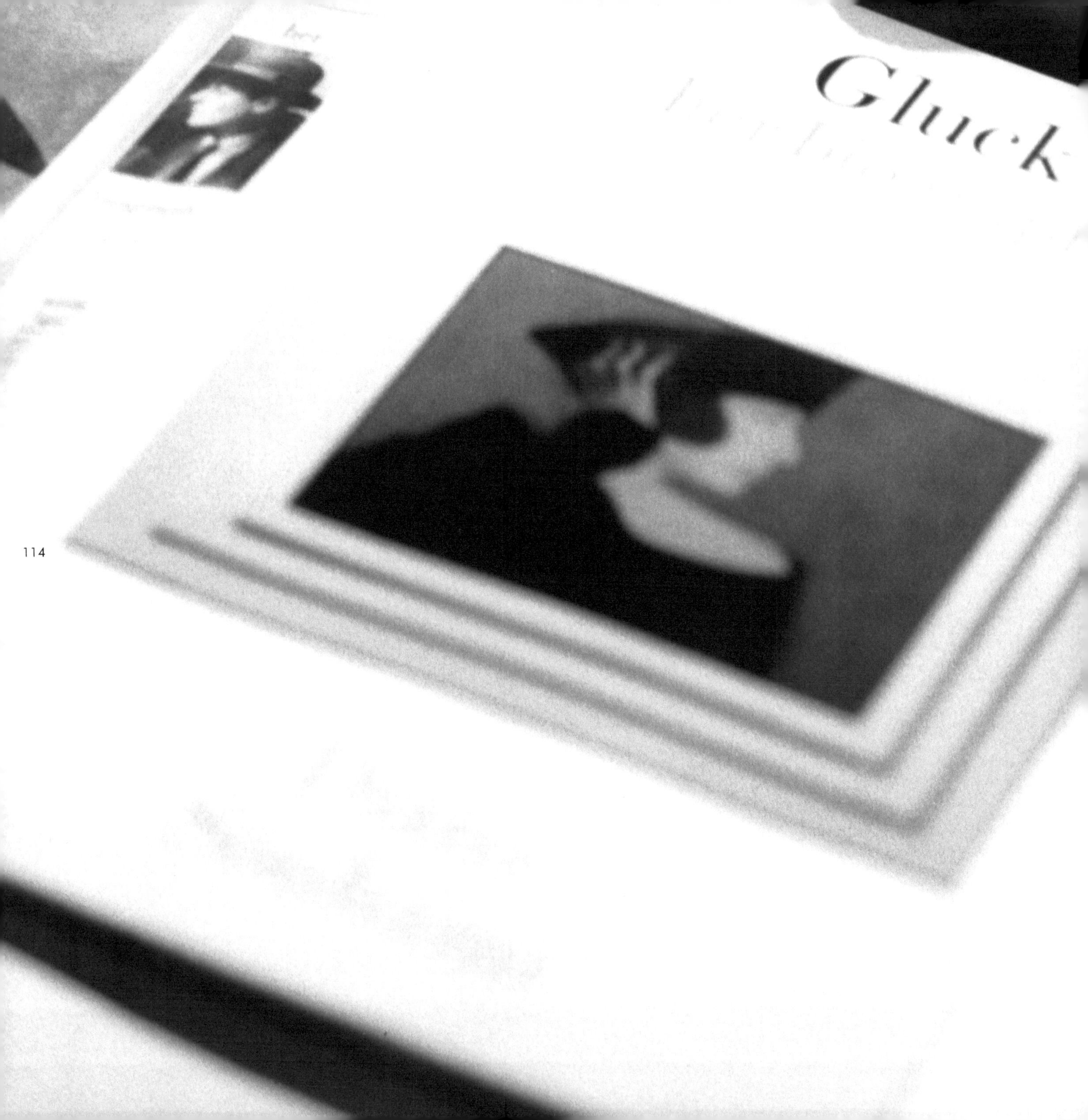
Gluck

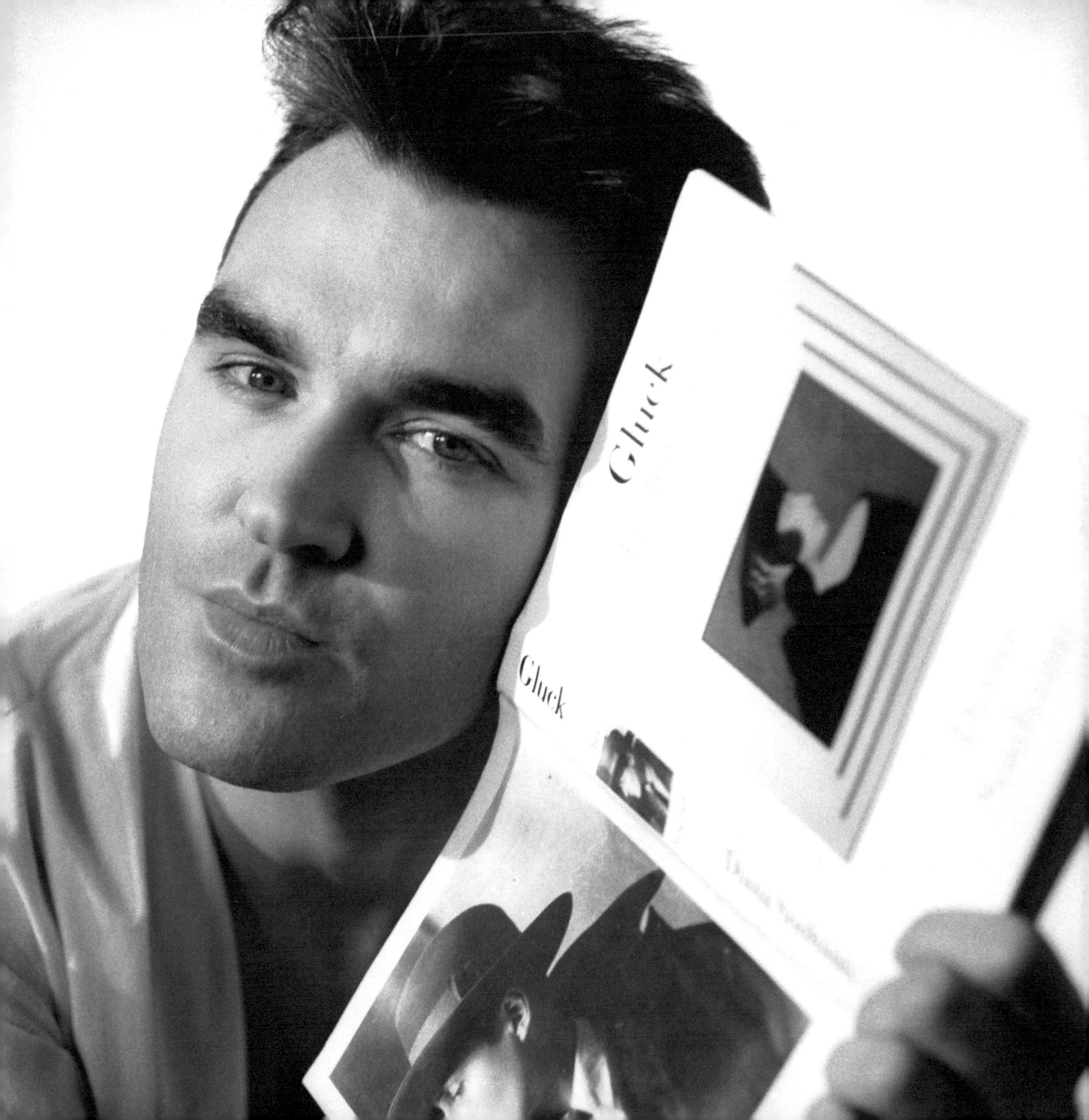
Gluck
Gluck

www.ingramcontent.com/pod-product-compliance
Lightning Source LLC
LaVergne TN
LVHW070215110826
845147LV00003B/577

9781905792450